ELLIOTT DURHAM
the Comprehensive School
on the hill

AND

ST ANNS
in inner-city
Nottingham

All Rights Reserved Worldwide

No part of this publication may be reproduced, stored in a retrieval system, or transmitted, in any form or by any means, electronic, mechanical, photocopying, recording or otherwise, without the prior permission of the publishers.

This book is distributed/sold subject to the condition that it shall not, by way of trade or otherwise, be lent, resold, hired out or otherwise circulated without the Pulisher's prior written consent in any form or binding or cover other than that in which it is published and without a similar condition including this condition being imposed on the subsequent recipient/publisher.

British Library CIP: a catalogue record for this book is available from the British Library

Copyright c Ruth I.Johns 1998

ISBN 0 9516960 2 5

Published 1998
PLOWRIGHT PRESS
P.O.BOX 66
WARWICK CV34 4XE

Order by direct mail from the Publisher or through a bookstore
Or ask your local library to obtain this book for you
(£6.50 post free UK)

Editor: Ruth I.Johns MA FIMgt, is a community historian, writer, and social innovator
Cover design: 3rd Millennium, Wellesbourne House, Wellesbourne
Printer: Warwick Printing Company Ltd, Warwick

DEDICATION

> To all students who attend inner-city schools. Don't believe negative criticisms which are put in your path without first looking at all the facts. Examine carefully the judgement of those whose view of a particular inner-city area is based on hearsay rather than knowledge. Have courage to make decisions which harness and develop your talents in all circumstances.

CONTENTS   Page

Editor's Introduction 1
Elliott Durham's first Headmaster by J.Wyndham Davies.......................... 8
Some of the happiest days of my life by Claire Pearson.......................... 16
Recollections from the school log book by Ian Johnson.......................... 19
I taught a class of more than fifty 8-year-olds by Kathleen Shaw.............. 23
Girls used needles to pierce their ears by Jill Ball................................... 27
I will always remember my first morning by Tony Cerabona...................... 28
The boys made Christmas cakes by Dorothy Wroughton......................... 30
I never really shone in anything by Jean Taylor...................................... 33
The offset litho knocked spots of the banda by Janet K.Saunders............. 37
New challenges by Matthew Ward... 41
An experiment in local history by Ruth I.Johns (including contributions by
Komal Pala and Claire Rogers).. 57
Anti-bullying peer counselling scheme (information from website)............. 63
Reflections of the current Head Teacher by Kathy Yates.......................... 69
Local history project (continued).. 70

Only named contributors are listed above. There are also many pages of photos, maps and information - past and present - about the school.

Front cover main photo: Year 11 students who left Elliott Durham Summer 1996. They particularly wanted a photo and the school decided to experiment to see if the costs could be recovered. Not enough were sold to make it a viable project to repeat. When money is tight in families, school photos are a luxury. This photo hangs in the school library. Below are 1997 details of the 1996 school leavers (*school information*).

DESTINATIONS FOR 1996 LEAVERS

6TH FORM COLLEGE	20.2%
FE COLLEGE	43.1%
YOUTH TRAINING (GET AHEAD)	9.2%
EMPLOYMENT WITH TRAINING	1.8%
EMPLOYMENT	6.4%
UNEMPLOYED	12.8%
UNAVAILABLE FOR WORK	3.7%
MOVED/NOT RESPONDING	2.8%

The photos on the inside of the front and back covers are some of the school's photo collection without captions/dates. They record aspects of school life over the years. Write to the address on the back cover if you can tell us more about any of these.

EDITOR'S INTRODUCTION

by Ruth I.Johns, community historian, who has had close connections with Elliott Durham in its early years and with St Anns since 1965. A few years ago, she became reacquainted with Elliott Durham. This publication is one result.

School history is important . . .

The history of any school, and of the community it serves, should be recorded.

Schools without a recorded history are at the mercy of current prejudice or myth. It is extraordinarily easy to ruin the reputation of a school when its history goes no further than individual memory or, even worse, individual or societal prejudice. For example, is it fair to judge a school mainly, or indeed solely, on its OFSTED* ratings published in the Press? Where is the access to other important information which depicts a school's strengths and weaknesses in assisting all its students to reach their potential, whatever their starting point?

Current and past school students need access to their school's history.

When applying for a job, those who have attended schools with a recorded history, such as traditional Grammar or Independent Schools and Public Schools, can be advantaged at a very early stage of the selection process.

Even if an individual detested 'their' school and excelled at very little whilst attending it, this corporate history can offer them advantages through life. We may (and I do) think that much about 'old school' networks is unfair. It is not the recording of history which is wrong, but that the advantages it bestows have been so little challenged or so little understood.

Comprehensive schools have been with us for many years now. If they were pieces of furniture they would have the status of 'antique!' Yet, too often, their history has not been well recorded or recorded at all. Elliott Durham's history has - until now - been almost totally unrecorded. This is not exceptional, especially for inner-city Comprehensive schools.

. . . and so is local history.

As a community historian, I am often reminded that, for many of us, interest in history is very local indeed. Thus, major events in history are accessed initially via personal and local interest. For example, the Second World War becomes history through people known personally who took part in it, whether in the Services or on the home front. And the history of housing is awakened through the lens of housing in a person's own locality.

An important aspect of British history which has never been acknowledged in terms of its impact on people's lives and their sense of destiny is the forced housing clearances of the late 1950's, the 1960's and early 1970's.

Thousands upon thousands of people and families were torn up from their roots and resettled often at considerable distance from them. It was assumed they would settle well and simply get on with their lives. Often, they were set down in areas which lacked community amenities and where they no longer had family and friendship links close by.

* Office for Standards in Education

Demolition of St Anns: a community abolished   *Nottingham Topic, September 1971*

St Anns, in Nottingham, was one such traumatised area. Some 30,000 people had to leave and eventually some 20,000 (mainly different) people returned to the 'new' St Anns. On page 28, Tony Cerebona mentions the hardship for his parents of having to leave a home they had so lovingly created in St Anns with a lot of effort.

Before it was redeveloped, there were many reasons why people from other areas came into St Anns, including some 650 shops [Tom Lynch, President of the Union of Small Shopkeepers, *Nottingham Post and News* interview 8.9.67] .These shops offered a wide range of products and services. Today very few 'outsiders' come into St Anns. Some professional people come to work in the area but seldom live in it.

Some of the 'tinned up" shops on St Anns Well Road (near Robin Hood Chase) await demolition

Nottingham Evening Post photo archive

St Anns was redeveloped largely between 1967-75. It still tends to live under the stigma typified by the Coates and Silburn study [this appeared in various publications including *Poverty: The Forgotten Englishmen*, Pelican, 1976]. The BBC film which followed the report, and made when St Anns was in its worst state of pre-redevelopment dereliction, is still deeply resented by some former St Annies. They feel it was unfair to equate being materially poor with being problem people.

Such has been the prejudiced reputation of St Anns that work-seeking adolescents are handicapped through their address. Or as one mother who lives near the Woodborough Road said to me: "My son puts Mapperley on his c.v. now because then he gets interviews."

In 1992, Kenneth Clarke, when Home Secretary, opened Anti-Drug Week in Nottingham. When asked which were the worst areas for drugs in Nottingham he responded instantly: "St Anns and Hyson Green." A colleague of mine on the local Press did not quote this because he felt it was yet another instance of the 'give a dog a bad name' syndrome.

February 1973, taken from cleared land at the top of Blue Bell Hill Road. St Anns Well Road runs along the bottom of the picture. The city is on the left. The caption to the photo read: "The replacement looks cleaner and tidier - only time will tell if this impression is to be a lasting one. The planners have done their part, and now it is up to the residents to re-instill the strong community spirit which was always very much part of St Anns." Nottingham Evening Post photo archive. [The scale and method of this type of community destruction was an injustice which has never been properly acknowledged. Whilst many of the poorly built inner terraces needed to go, the wholesale clearance included many well-built streets and houses and totally eradicated the known physical landscape. The knock-it-all-down-and-start-again policy was deemed cost effective, but who evaluated - or even considered - the social costs? Ed]

Personal contact with Elliott Durham.

My two sons, Martin and Neil, attended the school until we left Nottingham and have differing memories of it. One joined it as a Bilateral School, the other as a Comprehensive. Both went on to University. They are now in their late and mid 30's. Martin is a computer programmer. Neil is a father and a copywriter and publications consultant running his own business. My daughter, Naomi (1960-96, mother and, until she became terminally ill, Head of a Craft Design and Technology Department at a Sheffield inner-city Comprehensive school), was born between her brothers. She took the then standard 11+ exam. As a result, she attended Forest Fields Grammar School on the Carlton Road.

Most days, Naomi walked across St Anns to school and back. When the Comprehensive system was introduced, Forest Fields became a Sixth Form College. She and her peers were left in the tail of a dying Secondary School. It was only a few weeks before Neil started school that the Political decision to go Comprehensive was taken in Nottingham and he joined his brother at Elliott Durham rather than his sister at Forest Fields. They were confusing times for teachers, parents and children.

We lived on the Alexandra Park edge of St Anns during its years of redevelopment, and left Nottingham in July 1976. Until then, I also had close contact with Elliott Durham because its students were regularly involved with the Family First Trust, which I started in 1965 and for which I worked for over ten years. It helped to alleviate homelessness and isolation particularly of young people who were marginalised e.g. lone parents. At the end of 1973, I became a lone breadwinner parent myself.

Elliott Durham students' help at Family First was varied and included, for example, measuring, selecting and making the curtains for the flats in a newly converted Victorian house; assisting in child care; mending furniture and assisting at social functions. Family First offered practical projects about housing, design, building trades and ideas on DIY which introduced useful knowledge and skills for when students eventually set up home themselves.

I am remembered by the first Head Teacher of Elliott Durham (who writes on page 8) as a regular attender at Parents' Evenings, and for addressing School assembly about homelessness wearing a red mini skirt! (My knees were shaking)

Sometimes, Family First held events like It's a Knockout on Elliott Durham School premises, and for some years in the 1970's, it organised holiday play schemes at Elliott Durham School (see right).

Ever since leaving Nottingham in 1976, my work kept me returning to the city I love. A few years ago, I became a community historian. This enables me to stay in Nottingham (St Anns) several days a week.

I asked Kathy Yates, Head Teacher, if I could come into Elliott Durham and do some sessions with students on local history. I wanted to learn how much they knew about St Anns' history, and their views of their area. I was referred to Ian Johnson, Head of Humanities, who arranged weekly sessions in a Year

Individual's archive

HOLIDAY HOBBIES

A HOLIDAY hobbies scheme sponsored by Family First and run by Richard Stimson and his wife Christine was held at the Elliott Durham School during the Easter holidays and will be repeated for four weeks in the summer. The children catered for were in the five-13 age group. Activities included outings to Sherwood Zoo, Nottingham Castle and football, swimming, and art activities.
Pictured Gary Wormall (11) saves a penalty kick from Richard Stimson.

9 History class for five weeks on the understanding that students who were sufficiently interested could continue weekly lunchtime sessions with me until the end of term (9 weeks in total). He studied the School's log book to help this book (see page 19).

Six out of the 23 students who attended the classtime sessions for five weeks gave up time in their lunch hour to attend the local history group. This was encouraging considering the pull of football, chatting, and going out of school! This local history group did work in their own time, like visiting the local Library, keeping a diary and interviewing people (see pages 57 and 70).

Towards a recorded history of Elliott Durham.

My weekly sessions in Elliott Durham led to the idea for this book. Students were largely unaware of the history of St Anns, but keen to find out. Apart from its Log Book, there is virtually no accessible recorded history of Elliott Durham. It seemed sensible to start to fill this hole especially as the School plays a significant role in the life of the 'new' St Anns.

There are gaps in this book. For example, it needed more contributions from ex-students. It is sad that some, who are achieving a great deal, are reluctant to go on the record in association with the name of St Anns. This tells its own story about the loss of positive history.

Some interested people may not have known this book was in process. Letters in the Press asked for contributions. There were notices in Libraries and other public places. Many A4 leaflets (see below) were distributed via the school and in other places. But it is good that many people have co-operated in beginning to piece together the School's history.

Their contributions tell us much about changes imposed on the School from above (especially Matthew Ward's on page 41) and the changes in St Anns since the School started. The first Deputy Headmistress, Miss K. Shaw, was brought up in St Anns and remembers Empire Day being celebrated when she was a child (see page 23). By the time she joined Elliott Durham, its students increasingly were the children of families recently arrived from the Caribbean or from the countries of the Indian sub Continent.

DID YOU, OR DO YOU, GO TO THE

ELLIOTT DURHAM SCHOOL?

If you have ever been a pupil/student, teacher, office or ancillary worker at the School, at any time from its opening until now, please help to create a published history of the School.

Write something about your experiences of the school in as much detail as possible, and in any style you wish.

Imagine you are explaining to a relative in 200 years time what happened when you were at the school, and then tell your story in your own way.

Please remember to include the dates of the experiences, events etc about which you write. If you are/were a pupil/student, it would also be interesting to know how long your family has lived in the area, and whether you have had relatives attending the school.

PLEASE WRITE THE STORY WHICH ONLY YOU CAN TELL. SOME EVENT? SOME OCCASION? SOMETHING YOU LIKED, OR PERHAPS SOMETHING YOU DISLIKED? A DESCRIPTION OF SOME PART (OR ALL) OF THE SCHOOL? DESCRIBE LEAVING HOME FOR SCHOOL OR RETURNING HOME? WHICH SCHOOL DID YOU GO TO BEFORE? FAVOURITE SUBJECTS/ACTIVITIES? WHAT DID YOU DO AFTER LEAVING THE SCHOOL?

SEND YOUR WRITING TO: PLOWRIGHT PRESS

P.O. Box 66 Warwick CV34 4XE

Others, like new teacher Jill Ball (see page 27), were suprised to find themselves in a multi-racial school, marvelled at their own naivety and adapted quickly in a very positive way.

I remember only one teacher who was severely racially prejudiced in Elliott Durham's early years when discrimination in the workplace and in the private housing sector was still blatant. The School's ethos was one of equal opportunity.

Parents were often shy about attending School events like Parents' Evenings. They were sometimes criticised (see Chase Chat, St Anns community newspaper, June 1974). With hindsight, it is easy to understand how both indigenous parents newly moved into St Anns and parents newly arrived in the UK were diffident about the school system. Many had little experience of current Secondary education and were trying hard to build up their domestic and work lives, usually for the benefit of their children. Elliott Durham is on the (Mapperley) periphery of St Anns which does not facilitate access.

As in many other areas, the huge housing, economic and population changes in St Anns and the major changes to the education system created an inevitable division between school and home. Over the years, Elliott Durham teachers, parents and children have achieved much. And, out of the chaos caused by redevelopment, some real sense of community has emerged in St Anns. The people of St Anns are seldom affirmed for making mainly positive lives for themselves and their families, and for the community spirit which has been rebuilt despite a pot-pouri of circumstances which made it incredibly difficult.

Because staff are under such pressure, it is perhaps churlish of me to grumble that Elliott Durham's photos are an unsorted collection in a cardboard box: many without dates and captions. Some teachers told me they kept many photos for years and then sorted them and threw many away. But it is good to know that positive action (like now keeping all newscuttings about Elliott Durham) is in place to help keep an accessible record of school life. There are organisations with far greater resources than an inner-city Comprehensive school which are failing to keep proper archives (but that is another story!).

I end where I started by urging that recorded history for a school *is* necessary, as is knowledge of the history of the area which the school serves. Without this underpinning of knowledge of their school and local area, young people in St Anns - as in so many other areas - start with unfair disadvantage. They tend to hear their area discussed too often only in terms of crime statistics and lack of community. To combat this gross distortion of the facts, they need all the information available in order to take a balanced view. A recorded history - not to be confused with false nostalgia - is not just words on pages but a matter for discussion. It can help nurture a sense of personal and community identity which is valuable in all future eventualities.

The sample survey on page 59 indicates that Elliott Durham continues to play a pivotal role in the St Anns community. On page 69, Kathy Yates, Head Teacher, says it is the inner-city where she wants to stay.

Contributors to this book - in telling their recollections of Elliott Durham - also offer insights into social history. I leave readers to enjoy these without having them pointed out! I hope this book encourages more people to recall life and events about Elliott Durham which could be used in a later Edition. And I hope that other schools which have not recorded their history may be encouraged to do so. Community history is never static.

Material about Elliott Durham in local archives is sparse indeed. I could not even locate a copy of the special Nottingham Evening Post Elliott Durham supplement (see pages 55 and 66). The only complete record of newscuttings is the film archive of the Nottingham Evening Post held at the Local Studies Library, Central Library, on Angel Row. I did not have the time or eyesight to go through every issue since the school opened in 1966! I know there have been occasions in the past when local history projects have been undertaken in the school, including a local survey in 1967, but there is no trace of them.

I would be interested to receive a copy of their school magazine from inner-city Comprehensive schools which have one. Also, I would welcome first hand accounts from people who experienced enforced moves of home due to redevelopment. Did life for them and their families improve? Please send to the address on the back cover.

Thanks

My thanks to everyone who has contributed to or helped with this book in any way, including Kathy Yates, Head Teacher, for allowing me access to Elliott Durham; Ian Johnson, Head of Humanties, who saw the potential value to pupils of taking part in local history work and who offered considerable help; Lynne Fielding, School Librarian, for her help with photos and other relevant material; Teresa Gorecka at the Nottingham Evening Post photo archive which provided some of the photos: Anne Bott for checking the final draft and for making useful suggestions. Other photos were offered from individuals' personal archives and the sources are stated in so far as they are known; staff at the Local History Library, Central Library, Angel Row; Helen Blackmore, Community Librarian, and staff of St Anns Library. And, importantly, my thanks to students at Elliott Durham who enthusiastically recognised that we shared a common interest, and for their work, ideas and time which helped this project.

****

A 1967 photograph of Elliott Durham staff. No names were attached to the photo. People with knowledge of those times have filled in names. The result is not entirely satisfactory, but I hope any mistakes will be pointed out so - in the next Edition - all names will be completely accurate.

Back row (l to r): Andy Lee, Dave Kershaw, Trevor Parkin, Bill Norris, Brett Baines, John Rivers, Brian Hardy, Ken Hawkins, Malcolm Oram, Tony Thompson, Ivan Pegg, Roger Norman and Ron Price.

Second from back row (l to r): Grendon Hufton, Mike Pattison, Mrs. A.Craig, Bess Jenkins, Jill Ball, Ann Flanagan, Diane Vincent, Mrs Johal, Danny Corfield, and Bill Kerry.

Second from front row (l to r): John Bradshaw, Chris Gibson, ? , Joan Arscott, Dorothy Wroughton, Chris Mills, Muriel Longden, Nicki Walford, Hilary Caunt, Eileen Hartley, Kate Bond, Ruth Perkins , Pat Kenyon.

Front row (l to r): Ruth Nettleship, Linda Villette , Derek Kirk, Max Dobby, Ray Davies, Arthur Oswell, J. W. Davies (Headmaster), Kathleen Shaw, Keith Gordon, Mrs K. L. Robinson, Arthur Dalby-Phillips, Douggie Pitt, and Ann Goodall.

Inividual's archive

ELLIOTT DURHAM'S FIRST HEADMASTER, J.Wyndham Davies, describes some experiences of the School's early years.

Elliott Durham School, built on the old wartime gun site between The Coppice Hospital and Mapperley Hospital, was opened as a Bilateral School in September 1966. In 1974, it became a Comprehensive School. The School, named after Alderman Elliott Durham, Sheriff of Nottingham in 1966, gathered up pupils from three closing schools in the St Anns area: the Huntingdon Street Boys' School, Morley School, and the Sycamore Girls' School.

Incidentally, "Metz Durham" (as he was called) was a very interesting character. He served with the Canadian Expeditionary Force in World War One. He returned to Canada and married Alice. He was told he had six months to live. He decided to emigrate to England. He became a City Councillor, was Chairman of the Combined Police Authority and was Sheriff in 1966/67.

Building was still in progress when, in March 1966, I was appointed as the School's first Headmaster. Arthur Oswell was then appointed Deputy Headmaster and Miss Kathleen Shaw (from Sycamore Girls' School) was appointed Deputy Head Mistress.

At the time of these appointments, the new structure was taking place in a sea of mud and speculation. Speculation because the arrival of 1,000 pupils to the Mapperley area was bound to be a cultural and physical shock to its people who previously only had to put up with pupils from one small Junior School. The future was interesting!

What was to be the structure, the size of this new school? It was to have a separate House Block consisting of 6 dining areas, and 6 separate House Block rooms. In the Main Building were to be 31 classrooms, 2 metal work rooms, 2 art rooms, 4 science laboratories, a staff room, a big library, a main hall which would hold 825 seated pupils, and a magnificent 6,000 sq.ft. gymnasium. Of course, the Headmaster had his own rooms and the secretaries theirs.

Nottingham Evening Post 9.2.76
Local Studies Library, Angel Row

Outside there were 2 rugby pitches, 3 soccer pitches, tennis courts and a netball area.

While all this building was progressing, staff were being appointed and when the first staff meeting was called two days before the School's opening, there were 48 staff. It is interesting that 14 came from the schools that were closing (others, although given the opportunity, did not want to move to the new school) and a further 12 were brand new teachers. Not only were they coming to a brand new school, but they had never taught before! Some male teachers had never taught girls before and some female teachers had never taught boys. So, immediately, they had to change their attitutdes and it is to their credit that, given a few initial problems, they soon adjusted to the new situation.

Alderman Elliott Durham suggested to the Education Committee that 'his' school (he considered it 'his' school) should have its own swimming pool. This was not at first acceptable but, when he raised half the money required, the Committee fell in with his proposal and a swimming pool was built at the top of the drive. Soon after the school was opened, the swimming bath was filled. Something went dramatically wrong. Water poured down the drive, man-holes were ripped up and, before the water was turned off, the tennis courts and car parks in front of the school were flooded. Normality was soon resumed and nothing untoward has happened since.

Alderman Elliott Durham also suggested that he present a special book to the first person entering the school grounds. It was suggested that this would cause obvious problems on the first morning and, eventually, he presented books to the first Head Boy and Head Girl.

The School's emblem is the Maple Leaf which makes the connection with Alderman Elliott Durham who was Canadian.

The School opened on September 6th 1966 with 869 pupils. Mr. Oswell and I were at school at 7.30 a.m. to find the playground area full of pupils, not necessarily anxious to improve their educational potential, but anxious to see what their new school was like. All the pupils were in their correct forms by 9.15 a.m. when, lo and behold, the Director of Education arrived to see how things were progressing! He was told that everything was under control and he departed soon after!

However, a major fault in the organisation soon became apparent. At the 'old' schools, the toilets were outside. At the new School, they were inside. At 10.30 a.m. (time for break), 869 pupils poured out of the School searching for relief - and then ran back into the School. Break lasted 45 minutes whilst things were sorted out - surely the longest morning break in the history of Nottingham education!

The first months of work on the site of the Elliott Durham   *Individual's archive*

Yet another problem at lunch time! 621 pupils wanted to stay for dinner and could be accommodated physically but the kitchen ran out of plates and cutlery at 400. So 221 pupils waited in the playground for lunch, joined by those who had gone home for lunch and were now returning. A long lunch break too!

I was having my lunch of two potatoes and a slice of 'Fray Bentos' when the Secretary (Mrs D.Wroughton) told me that the Sheriff (Ald. Elliott Durham), the Sheriff's lady and the Chief Inspector of Schools (Mr Wall) had arrived! With my so-called lunch resting heavily on my stomach, I joined them in the School Hall where they chatted about the School, its

The Elliott Durham School Playing Fields (School in background) were created out of the side of the valley. Photo from City of Education Committee brochure for the offical opening of Elliott Durham, one of three city schools officially opened on 21.4.67. The others were Fernwood Infant and Southglade Junior and Infant Schools

facilities and future. At 3.40 p.m., I suggested that the party should leave as they would be crushed in the rush as 869 pupils dashed up the drive. Exhausted, but not disillusioned, I was heard to say: "Here endeth the First Day!"

The timetable for the first year was a 'holding' one. The staff did not know what the three closed down schools had achieved and what was the potential of the infinite variety of pupils coming from these schools. Incidentally, the construction of the timetable was not an easy task. My deputies and I had no rooms available yet in which to sit and ponder and much of it was done in the open air. We sat on two planks balanced on two empty oil-drums. This was a diagnostic year during which the standard and achievement of each pupil could be judged.

One important achievement came out of this year. The English Department found that five pupils from the Sycamore School were able to take G.C.E. "O" Level (by dint of hard work and commitment by girls and staff) and all five of them passed.

The staff responded to the new situation in a hard-working and co-operative fashion. Links were forged with a variety of organisations in the neighbourhood including the local Church, the Salvation Army and, most importantly, Family First. Also, by talking to local shop keepers, we hoped to soften the blow of having nearly 1,000 pupils invading the neighbourhood. This was not always successful, especially as so many pupils came to school on the 31 and 50 bus route with the resultant problems when they arrived and when they went home.

By January 1967, the number of pupils had risen to 1,030, the new arrivals being mainly from India and Pakistan. Just imagine how these children felt when, for instance, they could be living in a small hill village in India on Friday, could be flown by jet to England and arrive at School on a Monday morning. And their parents were so confident in the ability of their children to cope with these extraordinary changes! They would frequently bring them to School by bus in the morning and expect them to find their way home at 4.0 p.m.

Sport played a major part in bringing pupils from the three different 'old' schools together. Schools in the City co-operated in giving us games and most of the teams (cricket, rugby, soccer, netball) had full fixture lists. One amusing incident must be recorded. Our under-15 Rugby Team played a team from Nottingham High School. The opposition must have been unnerved by the size of some of the Elliott Durham forwards (mostly West Indians) and Elliott Durham won by 3 points to nil. And E.D. had the nerve to line up in two lines and clap the High School off the field!

The Official Opening of the School took place in April 1967 before an audience of pupils and parents. Councillors, the Chairman of the Governors and the Lord Mayor, the Sheriff and the Director of Education were on the platform. The Official Opening was preceded by a lunch at the Council House at which I was present. It was a colourful ceremony, pupils lining the stairs on the way to the Hall and the School Choir entertained the audience with a variety of songs.

I received a letter from the Director of Education congratulating the pupils on their demeanour at both ceremonies. The Elliott Durham School was now established as the major School in the area, its future was assured and many of its achievements in the future were due to the commitment of the staff and the attitude of most of the pupils.

When the School became a Comprehensive School in 1974, the Director of Education allowed me, along with other Head Teachers in the City, the freedom of organising 'our own settiing'. It meant that an individual pupil could attend the appropriate 'set' for his or her ability level in each subject. The first year was a diagnostic year, enabling me to judge the levels of ability the pupils had achieved in their Junior Schools. They were then put in 'sets' according to their ability in each subject.

When the School was a Bilateral School, before the introduction of comprehensive education, 28% of the City's children went to Grammar Schools and the next 22% were the top intake of the Bi-Lateral Schools. The lower part of the School had another chance to get into Grammar School education at the age of 13.

I am very proud to have been the first Headmaster of the Elliott Durham Comprehensive School. The pupils, mainly from St Anns, looked after 'their' School. Many of them have achieved a great deal in life and I was thrilled to meet 750 of them at the 25th Anniversary Celebrations.

The Gymnasium/Sports Hall of nearly 6,000 sq.ft. and the School Library. Photos from the City of Nottingham Education Committee's brochure for the Official School Opening

Ald. Elliott Durham, Sheriff of Nottingham, presents books to the head girl and boy at the Elliott Durham Bilateral School. (L to r) are Zena Armstrong, Robert Wakeling and the Sheriff

Individual's archive
Guardian Journal 8.9.66

Location plan of Elliott Durham and its playing fields.

From the current school brochure

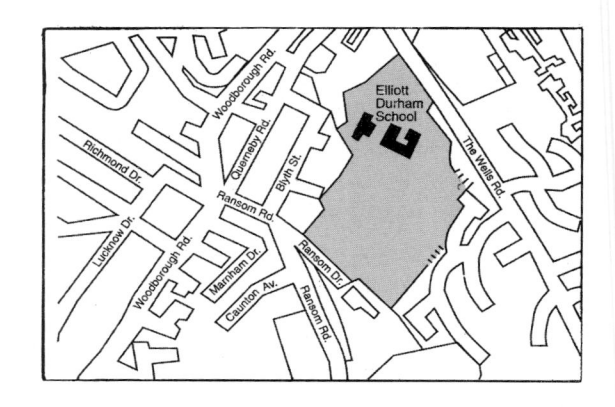

On the page opposite is a map of St Anns, 1956. The scale of this can only give an idea of the density of housing and commercial premises in the area, yet there is an abundance of nearby allotments. Anyone seriously interested in studying the changes to St Anns after redevelopment needs to study large maps (available at the Local Studies Library, Angel Row, Nottingham). Some of the 'old' street names have been reused - but not always in the same location! Note the empty space north of the allotment gardens above the Coppice Hospital in the right hand corner. It was in this space that the Elliott Durham was built.

In the small section of a 1980 map of the area (right), Elliott Durham is the school north of the Coppice Hospital. Note the extensive playing fields to the south of the School. The small playing field to the north of the School belongs to Walter Halls Primary School.

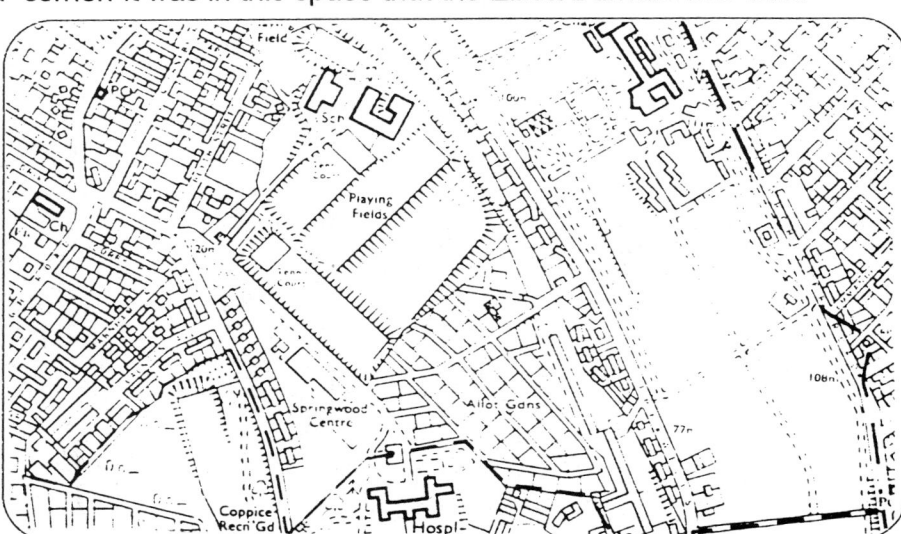

Courtesy Odnance Survey

12

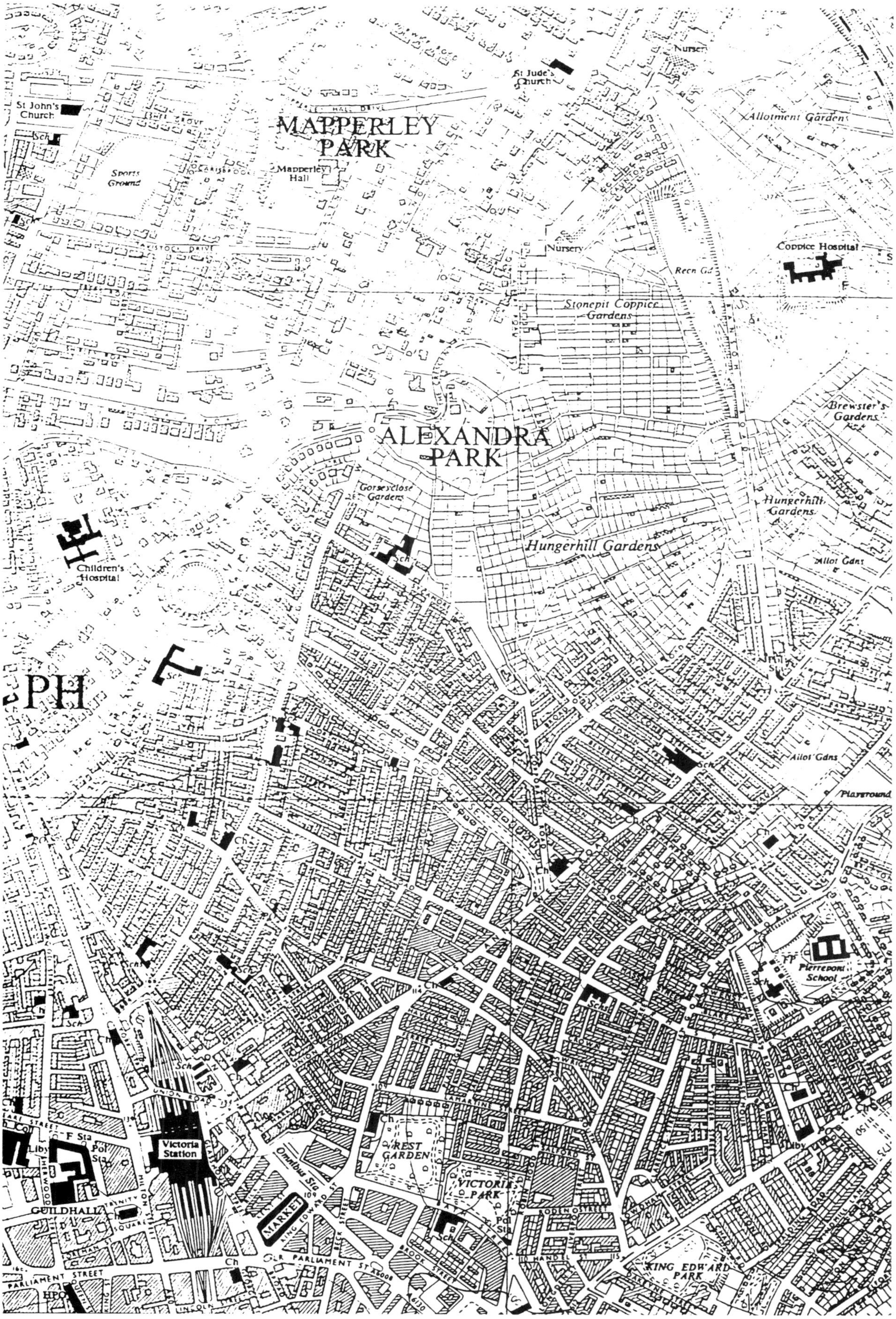

St John's Church
St Jude's Church
Nursery
MAPPERLEY PARK
Mapperley Hall
Sports Ground
Allotment Gardens
Nursery
Recn Gd
Coppice Hospital
Stonepit Coppice Gardens
Brewster's Gardens
ALEXANDRA PARK
Gorseyclose Gardens
Hungerhill Gardens
Hungerhill Gardens
Allot Gdns
Children's Hospital
PH
Allot Gdns
Playground
Pierrepont School
Victoria Station
F Sta
Pol Sta
Liby
GUILDHALL
REST GARDEN
VICTORIA PARK
MARKET
Omnibus Sta
KING EDWARD PARK
PARLIAMENT STREET
HPO

"The Elliott Durham Secondary School is the fulfilment of a policy of closing old, inadequate buildings and rehousing the pupils in well equipped new premises. In the past, the Huntingdon, Morley and Sycamore Secondary Schools have played a worthy part in the education of the children of the eastern area of the City but the new Elliott Durham School which replaced them provides the facilities necessary for the latter part of the 20th Century." From the City of Nottingham Education Committee's brochure for the official launch of the School. [The Elliott was certainly blessed with spaciousness. But it is interesting with hindsight to note how, in official comment, the role of teachers and teaching was not mentioned. Then, buildings were deemed the all important feature of a school. Today, it is OFSTED ratings. Maybe at some time in the future we shall get the balance right about what it means to provide a 'good' education? Ed]

Robert Cox (100 years old) was given a special tea party by members of the Mapperley Darby and Joan Club. He is cutting a cake baked by pupils of Elliott Durham School. He is helped by Mrs E.N.Jackson, club leader, and Mr.J.W.Davies, Headmaster of Elliott Durham

Individual's archive
Undated

ELLIOTT DURHAM SECONDARY SCHOOL

The school occupies an area of approximately 24 acres of steeply sloping land to the west of Ransom Road, Mapperley. The nature of the site posed special difficulties not only because it was necessary to create a series of plateaux to provide pitches with suitable levels but also because its upper part was used as a gun site during the last war and before building operations could commence it was necessary to demolish, by blasting, a number of concrete emplacements.

The premises of the school comprise the following :—

1. Assembly Hall and Gymnasia.
2. Main Teaching Block including Library.
3. Workshop and Teaching Block.
4. House Block on the Committee's accepted pattern including Kitchen and House dining areas and club rooms.

The standard form of construction is steel frame cased in fair faced concrete with brick in-filling walls. Perhaps the most interesting feature of the accommodation is the gymnasium/games hall of nearly six thousand square feet which can be used either as a single area or divided by sliding folding full height doors to provide two gymnasia of standard size.

Contractors :	Buildings :	J. Searson, Ltd., Sutton-in-Ashfield, Notts.
	Playing Fields :	En Tout Cas Co. Ltd., Syston, Leicester.
Cost :	£453,096.	
Cost of furniture, apparatus and equipment, including school meals	£63,165.	
Erection commenced :	Playing fields :	September 1962.
	Buildings :	July 1963.
School first occupied :	September 1966.	

From the City of Nottingham Education Committee's brochure for the official launch of Elliott Durham

GOVERNORS OF THE
ELLIOTT DURHAM SECONDARY BILATERAL SCHOOL

COUNCILLOR C. BENNETT, Chairman,
G. W. EDWARDS, ESQ., Vice-Chairman,

COUNCILLOR O. BARNETT, B.E.M., M.A., J.P.,
COUNCILLOR P. M. LYNCH,
COUNCILLOR MRS. O. M. MOSS,
COUNCILLOR A. H. JOHNSON,
MRS. M. K. FISHER,

F. J. NEALE, ESQ.,
R. SPENDLOVE, ESQ.,
C. J. SWIFT, ESQ.,
A. J. WILLCOCKS, ESQ., B.Com., Ph.D.,
S. B. WINNING, ESQ.

School governors at the time of the official school launch 1967

Friday May 31st, to Friday June 7th, 1968

ELLIOTT DURHAM BILATERAL SCHOOL
J.W. Davies B.A.   Headmaster.

WHITSUNTIDE JOURNEY

OSTEND
NANCY
BASLE
BERNE
GENEVA
MONTREUX

With the exception of the extracts from Matthew Ward's degree thesis, all named material in this book is written especially for it [1994-96] by people with first hand experience. If you have any recollections of Elliott Durham, between 1966 and now, to add to what appears in these pages, please write them down and send them (with photos if you have relevant ones) to the address on the back cover. If you attended Elliott Durham, please also let us know what you have done since leaving school.

Recollections of the same events vary and this adds authenticity. Truth is never wrapped in one person's memory, nor even in official records. We work toward an understanding of our past through common experience openly shared from different perspectives. Ed.

Elliott Durham photo

ELLIOTT DURHAM SCHOOL
1967-68
UNDER 15 TEAM

15

SOME OF THE HAPPIEST DAYS OF MY LIFE, says Claire Pearson (nee Johnson), who attended Elliott Durham 1967-72.

Prior to attending the School during the early days, I can remember it being built.

We lived on Mapperley Top, and I had an Auntie who lived down the Wells Road. Her back garden was directly opposite the old railway embankment from which the School appeared to tower against the skyline. I can remember with fascination looking on as the School began to take shape. I would have been about 8 or 9.

Later on, when I was a First Year, the junior girls' playground was more or less directly opposite her back garden, separated by the embankment and railway cutting. I remember waving to her, when she used to hang her washing out, from my vantage point of being higher up.

I attended with my niece (my eldest sister's daughter) who is the same age as myself. We all lived together then with my parents. There was a close-knit group of friends who lived nearby and we used to meet up en route to school. We were considered posh by our peers at the School because of where we lived at the time.

The School was classed as a Secondary Bilateral School and was very modern for its time. I remember the smell of newness: wood, paper, polish with a faintly antiseptic tinge to it. I am a Registered Nurse now working in a new hospital and some of the rooms there have the same smell about them. It takes me back every time to my first days at the 'big' School.

During the first few years, the girls and boys were segregated during break times. The boys had the lower playground and the girls the upper one. Lo and behold if you were ever caught in the wrong one!

During my Third Year, I went on the annual School trip to Belgium along with some of my friends. I begged and pleaded with my Mother who eventually gave in and gave me £1 a week to take in toward the cost. I think the total cost of the holiday only came to about £28.

Mr Derek Kirk, the music teacher, was in charge of the trip. He was one of the strict teachers. What an adventure it was. One of our first tastes of freedom despite the teachers who supervised as parents in loco.

Off we all went on the Hovercraft. There were five of us in our room. What a time we had in our Seventies' flares and piling on the seventies look make-up. There were day trips to Bruges and Ghent, and going to the local disco in the evening and dancing to the then banned French song Je t'aime.

I cannot remember the exact year. I was about 15. A local television company made a documentary film called A Way of Life. It centered around a group of young adults who lived in the St Anns area on Bluebell Hill. They had set up a Community Centre for residents of the area, young and old.

The School was involved in the making of the film because many pupils lived in St Anns. My Year was particularly involved and included in the filming. So, some teachers, peers and myself appeared in the documentary which went out on national T.V.

I remember my English teacher, Mr. Robert Howard and 'Potty' Mr. Roger Norman, the Art teacher. They were friends and one year put on a School play. Mr. Norman played the guitar in one scene and persuaded me to sing a solo which they had composed. To this day, I can still feel the utter mortification of having to do that song in front of the School.

Talking of singing, a group of us were in the School Choir: Pamela, Cheryl, Janet, Bonnie [her family nickname, also known as Thelma], Alinka, Brenda, myself. Initially, we managed to get in thinking, wrongly, it would be an easy option. How wrong we all were! Mr. Kirk would make us practise, practise, practise: usually after School hours. One year, we did the Gilbert and Sullivan Opera, The Pirates of Penzance. That was a success. We also used to sing at the local church at Christmas time plus the School's Carol Service.

The Needlework Department one year put on a fashion show. I vaguely recollect that one of the fashion companies was also involved. Along with a few other girls, I was chosen to model some of the clothes, probably because we were tall, apart from one of my closest friends, Linda, who was under 5 foot. She had to model all the girlish designs much to her utter disgust and contempt.

During the earlier years, tights had not caught on and us girls still wore sheer stockings held up with stretchy girdles. And, of course, the mini skirt was in fashion: first time around. We used to roll our pleated skirts up above our knees. The inevitable always happened with stockings starting to slip down. The lads would shout and whistle: "Hoy! Your stocking tops are showing."

Mr.J.W.Davies was the Headmaster then and Miss K.M.Shaw was the girls' Headmistress and Deputy Head: one of the old school. She used to teach at the Girls' Sycamore School before. If either of them entered a class whilst a lesson was in progress, the whole class would stand up from their desks.

I remember the House Blocks. I imagine, they are still the same: Lawrence, Hudson, Ottawa, Vancouver and Toronto. Each one was colour coded and we would wear our coloured badges on our blazers or jumpers. Mine was orange (Lawrence).

Then, they were strict about uniform. Mid-blue shirts, navy skirts and cardigans. Red, yellow and orange stripe ties. Of course, we always tried to deviate slightly in some way!

I was in the girls' hockey team until I started studying for my exams. We never seemed to win any matches then. All I can remember, it seems, is running about on freezing cold, windswept playing fields getting bruised legs. We used to wear short red skirts and white Airtex T-shirts. Mind you, I remember once during some inter-house games, Lawrence won the trophy for that year in hockey. It was probably because a few of us were in the School hockey team.

The Swimming Baths were built at the top of the drive. It was something to boast about that your School had its own Swimming Bath. Funnily enough, I can never remember going there very often, although I'm sure we did.

I remember Mr Pitt, a science teacher and Miss Kenyan the maths teacher who totally gave up on me at one point. Maths still is my weakest point although I am better than I was.

I remember my Mother used to say: "One day you'll look back and these schooldays will be the happiest of your life." Well, 24 years on, you can imagine a lot has happened in my life. I have travelled extensively worldwide, I have a career and my own home. I've had tears of happiness and great sorrow, and met many wonderful - and not so wonderful - people. My best and closest friend still is one of my school friends. We see each other often and, strangely enough, my niece is now in contact with another close school friend who I met up with again a few months ago. We hadn't seen each other since we were 16 and on our last day at school.

I loved my last years at school and didn't want to leave when the time came. Then, unemployment wasn't the problem it is now. Jobs were easier to come by. I didn't enter my nurse training until I was 19. The time after leaving school till then was full of studying and having jobs to earn me money.

I do look back and think what Mum used to say. And, yes, I would say those days were some of the happiest of my life. Sometimes they seem only yesterday and it's hard to believe it was over 20 years ago since I last walked through those school gates on Querneby Road/Blythe Street into the unknown.

Putting the finishing touches to The Maple (also see page 22). Teacher Bohdan Dziedzan with (l to r) Rhoda Troon, Mark Devos, Fina Chibbaro and Samantha McKenzie

Nottingham Evening Post photo archive. Undated

Senior Captain: Sonia Watts. Junior Captain: Michelle Bowler   *Elliott Durham photo*

RECOLLECTIONS FROM THE SCHOOL'S LOG BOOK, and from people involved with the School, by Ian Johnson, Head of Humanities.

A School which grew out of an area used for a tip and a World War Two gun site, populated by wild flowers, is still serving the community of St Anns thirty years later. The School was built in four years and named after the Canadian born Sheriff, Alderman Elliott Durham. Its opening was proclaimed as a 'Day of Pride for City Educationalists'.

It was first named the Elliott Durham Bilateral School and its opening was a proud moment for the Alderman, seen here looking out over the School playing fields with (top) Mr. J. W. Davies, the first Headmaster, Mr. K. Wall (Chief Inspector of Schools) and the Sheriff's lady, Mrs Durham.

The National Anthem was sung and the School Choir sang You Gotta Get Glory by Arnold Williams. Thirty years later, one wonders what would be sung if the School were to open now. One also wonders if the opening words spoken by Alderman Durham are still pertinent to the present pupils of the School:

"I would be happy if all you can learn is to be honest upright citizens of this marvellous city, then you can be proud of your School and I will be very proud indeed of you."

Guardian Journal 8.9.66
Local Studies Library, Angel Row

The history of the School with its pupils starts on September 2nd 1966. The Headmaster, Mr J. W. Davies marched down the drive with 45 members of staff and 886 pupils, 449 boys and 437 girls. The Sheriff visited the School on the first day and presented books to the Head Boy and Girl, Robert Wakeling and Zena Armstrong (photo page 12).

The pupils had arrived from Sycamore Girls' School, two boys' schools - Huntingdon and Morley - and first year pupils from the local feeder Primary School. There was many a disagreement between the older boys and a particularly nasty one between two fourth year girls in the shower (I will leave the rest to the imagination).

On the first day, 886 pupils rushed out into the yard at break, only to rush straight back in again when they realised that the toilets were actually inside the building. School dinners did not finish until half an hour after the start of afternoon school because there had been a shortage of cutlery.

A year later the roll of the School had risen to 1,008 pupils and 8 more staff.

One of the saddest stories of the early years was that of a boy who went from the first year to the fourth without anyone believing his age. When he reached the fourth year, it was officially confirmed that he was only 11 years old and he had to go back to the first year and start again.

Many of the pupils who have passed through the gates have been an excellent advertisement for the School and for St Anns. There have been numerous sporting achievements both in team sports and individually. Past pupil Loreen Hall became English Schools Champion and was at one time ranked number two in the U.K. Athletics has always been a strong tradition at the School with the girls winning the City Athletics shield for the first time in May 1979. The boys followed that success, reaching the North Eastern section of the National Schools Athletics Championships in June 1983.

More recently, football has dominated with the Under-16 boys winning the City Cup in 1983 and then winning the Forest Bowl in 1990. In the last two years, the Under-16 boys and the Under-13 girls have won 5-a-side football tournaments in Nottingham and gone on to represent the County in national competitions. In the earlier days of the School, the staff also got in on the act with John Pallant representing England at Rugby Union against Ireland and then France in 1967.

The redevelopment of St Anns in the late 1960s and early 1970s caused many problems for the School. Children at School on the Friday were not there on the Monday and vice versa. Some returned, some did not. The excellent community spirit that existed in the old St Anns was very quickly lost as the area was redeveloped and 'improved.' Consequently, the School and its pupils lost out as the new St Anns did not develop the same sense of community.

Loreen Hall
Individual's archive

During this period, the School developed a close link with the Family First organisation, which led to the first-ever Work Experience with about 40 pupils going out every Thursday afternoon. At the time, this was a relatively new departure for a Secondary School.

The atmosphere at School was much less stressful for staff and pupils in the 'good old days.' There are examples of the first Headmaster, Mr Davies, covering for staff so that they could travel and watch a Forest away match. With all the pressures of the National Curriculum and so few teachers available to cover as a result of staff cuts it would be highly unlikely for this to happen today.

This more relaxed approach provided for a more relaxed relationship between staff and pupils resulting in the odd sports fixture between staff and pupils, although the atmosphere does not always seem to have been good, as the record of one of the first Rugby matches shows. The match was stopped at half time beause the staff were being too violent!

With cricket, it was different. Was it because there was no physical contact or was it because the staff were always bound to win in the early days because they had the luxury of Mr Davies, an ex-County player from Glamorgan! Surprisingly, the staff never lost.

Soccer was an opportuntiy for pupils to get their own back, usually giving the staff a good run for their money, until those matches were stopped in the 1980s after a teacher broke his leg. There was a funny side to the story.

A boy had been put on detention that evening and had been made to stand and watch the match as part of the detention. As the member of staff was carried into the ambulance, he felt obliged to say: "Sir, can I go now?" The reply, as they say, is lost to history.

Of course, relationships with the outside world have not always been perfect. The first time the School was repainted, one of the painters made unsavoury comments about the colour of a pupil's skin and his parentage. The painter refused to leave and his boss had to come to the School and sack him before he would leave. There was also the incident with the local man coming down the School drive armed with a scythe, accusing pupils of damaging his allotment. Thankfully, he didn't get the opportunity to meet the pupils in person.

An essential part of a school is the extra curricular activities it provides for its pupils and the link it has with the community. In the early days, there are records of trips to the Albert Hall to see the Birmingham Symphony Orchestra and the Band of the Royal Marine Guards. A far cry from the visit of teenage pop idol Peter Andre who visited the School recently.

In 1972, there was even a visit by 80 pupils to the Ballet at the Theatre Royal. Today, there are regular trips to the Theatre on a Monday night (free tickets permitting!) by pupils from Years Ten and Eleven.

School visits abroad have included Holland, Belgium and France (to see the Bastille celebrations) as well as the 'traditional' School skiing trip (no broken legs reported in the School Log Book!).

Throughout the 1980s and early 1990s school camps were a very important aspect of School life with camps to the Lake District, Rutland Water, Wales and Derbyshire. Many lament the demise of camps but, as costs rise, they have become less viable. Fortunately, some pupils have been able to participate in recent camps to France. These trips seem to pass without too much incident, although the School Log Book does record a very harrowing time on the London Underground counting the pupils on and off at each stop.

It also records the time when, worried by the brakes on a bus, one member of staff felt he had to report it to the Police who proceeded to take the bus off the road for faulty brakes!

The Amateur Dramatics of pupils have not always been confined to visits abroad or indeed the classroom! There is a strong tradition of School productions: Oliver! in 1985, Bugsy Malone in 1989, Guys and Dolls in 1991, Man of Steel in 1992, Rock Solid in 1993 and finally Grease in 1996.

Links with the community have always been important and the School Log Book refers to many social functions which sadly have not been as numerous recently. Perhaps it is time for the School and its community to rekindle the links and go forward together.

There have been highs and lows to the School/Community relationship. The meeting to Save our Schools in 1977 where nobody turned up was obviously a low point! On a more positive note, there were Staff v Parents sports fixtures especially the Staff v Parents Cricket Match in 1968 with the staff running out winners by three wickets (having the assistance of an ex-County player from Glamorgan!)

The School has always been willing to give time to the community. Throughout the 1970s there were numerous parties for local O.A.Ps, and various School Fairs to raise money for the School Fund and new mini bus. In 1984, there was an Elliott Durham supplement in the Nottingham Evening Post, in which in 1985 there was a report highlighting the new Nature Area.

More recently, pupils from the School have regularly given concerts at the local Springwood Centre. The pupils have also managed to raise considerable amounts of money for charities over the years, ranging from the Aberfan disaster in 1966 to the Blue Peter Appeal in 1990. More recently, fund raising has been focussed on a sponsored swim by a teacher at the School to send a team to the Paralympics in Atlanta.

Pupil numbers at the School have fluctuated over the years, reaching a peak of over a thousand in the 1960s and now settled at approximately 500, a good number which enables staff to keep in touch with their pupils. The School has also suffered many interruptions and closures. Government 'initiatives' have meant massive changes to School life and subjects taught.

The pressure that comes with these changes almost invariably means a change in atmosphere of the School as pressure builds on staff and pupils alike. Throughout the 1970s, the School was disrupted by strikes by either teachers, caretakers or even pupils in 1978. The latter led to the Police being called and the ring leaders suspended.

The late 1980s and early 1990s have seen dispruption as a result of interference by central Government. School has also been disrupted by numerous boiler problems, the usual burst pipes, the odd dead rat found in a heater, Princess Anne's wedding, a couple of bomb threats and, on a sombre note, the funeral of the School's namesake, Alderman Elliott Durham, on February 13th 1976.

Hopefully, the School will continue to develop over the next thirty years, no doubt rising to the challenges set and responding to the needs of its pupils and the community of St Anns.

****

There have been attempts at running a school magazine from time to time. The only copy which has been found so far is the second edition of *The Maple* (also see page 18) which includes the item below:-

"No doubt everyone is becoming aware of the preparations for the spectacular musical 'Oliver!' A cast of over 50 pupils and staff have been rehearsing songs and acting, aiming for presentation on the 6th, 7th, 8th February 1985. And there is every sign that it will be a show worth seeing.

"It has been amazing to discover the depth of talent among the cast, ranging from the singing of the workhouse paupers and Fagin's gang to the individual acting, singing and dancing of the well-known characters, Fagin, Bill Sykes, Nancy, Oliver and the Artful Dodger.

"There is still a lot of work to be done and long hours spent after school rehearsing for the show. But everyone seems to be enjoying it! One pupil even gave up a lucrative paper round job to be in the show. So after all this effort - won't you make an effort to come and see it. We'll expect you."

A scene from Oliver!
Elliott Durham photo

I TAUGHT A CLASS OF MORE THAN FIFTY 8-YEAR-OLDS,

says Kathleen Shaw of her first teaching post in St Anns, where she was born in 1916, and lived and worked there until around 1945. In 1960, she returned to teach English and Music at the Sycamore Girls' School in St Anns, and in 1966, became Elliott Durham's first Deputy Headmistress until she retired in 1976. Miss Shaw's name appears in several people's recollections of Elliott Durham in this book. Here she tells us something of the St Anns of her early years.

My father was born in Nottingham in 1886 and was a Master Plumber. My mother's family were a middle class family from Swaffham in Norfolk. She was born in 1888. They had four children of whom I was the eldest and the only girl. We were all educated until we were eleven at the Sycamore Junior School. We passed the Scholarship exam to Mundella Grammar School. Afterwards, I went to Derby Teacher Training College. One brother became a teacher after Army service; one a professional photographer after serving with the RAF as Flight Lieutenant, and one a professional musician - singer and conductor - after Army service.

The schools' system of my childhood now seems prehistoric, and yet the basics of education were thoroughly taught and I cannot remember any of my classmates being unable to read and write. I started my education at the Sycamore Infants' School in St Anns. Although we worked very hard, there were memorable occasions which stick in my mind. The Headmaster, supposedly as a treat, used to gather a great crowd of rather smelly boys and girls into a large room which was stepped like a lecture hall and give us a lantern lecture. In the dark and in that great crowd I was rigid with terror especially when the oxygen tubes began to hiss and I expected a huge explosion. But I survived!

A much happier memory is of Empire Day. Everyone took part. From somewhere, mothers produced costumes showing the dress of all countries of the Empire. There was a Maypole, and the boys did the sword dance for which they were famous (a tradition which survived in the St Anns Well Road until at least 1966). They were happy and innocent days. I must have progressed fairly well for when I passed on to the Big School I got good marks and eventually passed the Scholarship.

There were active and lively groups such a Guides, Scouts, Cubs, Brownies, Boys' Brigade, Girls' Life Brigade and, of course, the Churches and Chapels. My Church was St Anns, now sadly demolished. It was a beautiful 19th Century building on the St Anns Well Road near the bottom of Robin Hood Chase. The Church School was my first teaching post.

St Anns' Church demolition

Nottingham Evening Post photo archive

I had a class of more than fifty 8-year-olds, all of whom could read and write and do sums.

The Church was crowded every Sunday night and, once a month, all the youth organisations attended Matins in smart uniforms with banners and much ceremony. On Whit Sunday, they and the Sunday School pupils had a huge parade through the streeets of the Parish, everyone wearing something new and looking very smart. The various bands led us and we stopped from time to time to sing hymns before going to Church for a service. There must have been participants from the Chapels too. They were well attended every Sunday and had huge Sunday Schools and enjoyed lavish Anniversaries when children performed songs and readings. It was all very jolly and friendly.

I must mention The Mission. This was a sturdy building at the bottom of the Coppice (now Ransome) Road where - for years - my uncle, Mr. Charles Harper, conducted Sunday night services which consisted of rousing choruses and short talks. They were so popular that you had to be there an hour before the service to be sure of getting in.

Next door to The Mission was a smaller building where a Club for the menfolk, called The Institute, was held. This was the only provision for men that I knew of. The ladies had various sewing meetings and Ladies' Guilds, but my mother was too busy to attend these so I knew very little about them.

There was a wonderful body of men, all keen allotment gardeners, who grew the most astonishing selection of flowers and vegetables, and who organised the St Anns' Rose Show every year. This was held on 'Coppice Rec' (the Coppice Road Recreation Ground) and was centred on a display of produce, especially roses, in a marquee. To us it was a joy because there were also side-shows and stalls etc: wonderful!

The Roman Catholics kept themselves to themselves and I unfortunately knew nothing about them. On Cranmer Street, there was a large building which housed the Gordon Boys' Home. This was a charity for homeless boys and named after General Gordon. The boys used to wear a quasi-military uniform (very thick and hot in Summer) and with very heavy boots. They used to go about in a squad, marching everywhere to go to work or jobs. I was very sorry for them.

The Salvation Army, on the edge of the area, was active in helping the poor and sick. All of the above organisations were, of course, self-supporting. They received no funds or grants from the Government. Generally speaking as children we amused ourselves.

Until the post-war rebuilding, there was no such place as 'St Anns'. The area now known as St Anns consisted of three main areas, all virtually foreign territory to each other. I was born on Hungerhill Road and never set foot on the opposite side of St Anns Well Road until my late teens, and the area from [the then] Hungerhill Road to Woodborough Road was quite unknown to us except for Sycamore Road.

Doomed houses in Hungerhill Road await demolition. In the foreground is a handcart belonging to one of the gangs travelling around the area turning off power supplies

Nottingham Evening Post photo archive

Miss Kathleen Shaw retired at the end of the Summer Term 1976. Here, she is showing the gold watch she received to the Lord Mayor of Nottingham, Councillor Stan Rushton (right), a governor of the school. The watch was presented to her by the Head Teacher, Mr.J.W.Davies (left) on belhalf of staff and colleagues. Also looking on are departmental heads, Mr.G.Senior and Mr.P.Cole.   Nottingham Evening Post photo archive 16.7.76

The main artery of the area was St Anns Well Road, running from the junction of Wells Road and Coppice Road (now Ransome Road) and ending more or less at The Square, where it was crossed by Alfred Street North and Alfred Street South. It was said that you could be born on St Anns Well Road and live your whole life there until you were taken off by Bamfords Funeral Service without ever leaving the road. There were shops and services catering for every need and occasion: food shops of every description, shoe shops, clothing shops, dairies, pawn shops (much patronised on Monday mornings), furniture shops, photographers, newsagents, tobacconists, beer-offs, funeral directors, The Welcome (more of which later), chemists: I could go on.

Running down to St Anns Well Road on both sides were numerous side streets. Every one had at least one and sometimes three small shops, two at the top corners and one half way down. The whole area was always busy, thronged with people, though many of the shops ran on credit and most people had very little to spend. There were no family allowances, free school meals etc. But much money was spent on beer!

As a child living on the edge of the area, I was not knowledgeable about social conditions of the time. But I was necessarily aware of the conditions in which many people lived. Each side street had areas of terraced houses running off on each side and it was here that conditions were dreadful. There were no lavatories or bathrooms and usually only a sink in the kitchen with a cold tap. Some houses only had a common tap outside. The houses ran, sometimes back to back, with a long communal yard in front for about 50 yards, with a 'privy' for each house, the tub in which was emptied once a week.

The condition of these houses was very poor. Considering all this, it was amazing that the spirit of the people was so uncomplaining and stalwart and that they found fun and enjoyment wherever they could. There were fights and wife-beatings but anyone in trouble would be helped and the Saturday night drunks were very understandingly dealt with. There was a rare gallery of eccentrics in the street I knew best, Westminster Street. The people, although rough and little educated, had wit, individuality and independence. Of course, there were strong family links which kept the community together.

One cannot suppose that children brought up in such poor housing conditions would be brimming over with good health, but, surprisingly, they were not thin, starved looking waifs and most were lively and sturdy. It is not true they went bare foot and ragged. I never saw children without shoes or boots. The boys usually wore heavy boots with studs. Often clothes and footware were passed down in the family but all but the very poorest were able to turn out on special occasions looking neat and clean.

I am not clear about provisions for health care, since we were lucky enough to go privately to a doctor (2/6 a visit), but there was something called The Panel on which most people depended although the doctor was called upon in serious cases. On Commercial Square, St Anns Well Road, was an institution called The Welcome. It was many years before I realised that this sign came from the name above the entrance which read Mothers and Babies Welcome. Who ran this, I do not know. But in those days before the National Health Service, Social Security, Family Allowances and so on, it was a great boon to mothers who received advice on baby care, family health and their own health. They were able to bring their babies to be checked, weighed and generally looked after without charge.

There were, of course, a number of doctors in the area, working single-handed in their own practice and quite accustomed to being called out in the night after a full day's work: no relief doctors then!

There were the hospitals for Nottingham, of course. The General was the most important, followed by a small City Hospital which included an Isolation Block. I once spent a month there in a widespread Scarlet Fever outbreak. Then there was the Women's Hospital on Peel Street and the Children's Hospital near Mansfield Road.

All the above were observations of a child and not very interested teenager. I know that in a teaching post I had at St. Mary's Church Senior School in the Lace Market, there was a considerable amount of TB and, no doubt, this was also to be found in St Anns.

Incidentally, the name Wells Road refers to the fact that the land covered by the Elliott Durham School and playing fields was (and probably still is) riddled with wells. No wonder we had floods in bad weather! St Anns is a very interesting area, for it was reputed to have been a King's hunting ground centuries ago. Whether true or not, this story must have had some basis in fact. The area in the story is that of the St Anns allotments, alongside Hungerhill Road, which are very old and seemingly unchanged for at least a hundred years.

The name St Anns Well Road is a reminder of an actual well which was situated at the junction of the present St Anns Well Road and Ransome Road and which was in times past regarded as holy and an object of pilgrimage.

St Anns Well in Victorian times

GIRLS USED NEEDLES TO PIERCE THEIR EARS, says Jill Ball (nee Rougeault), who taught at Elliott Durham 1966-71.

I was accepted into the Nottingham Pool of Teachers in 1966 (as a newly qualified teacher) and I was told I had a job in a new school. I went to Mr. Davies', the Headmaster's, house in Trowell for an interview. I couldn't believe he was the Head as we had such a laugh!

On our first day, I could not believe the number of staff in the staffroom.

It was the most wonderful start to my career. Experienced teachers were asking me where rooms were! When the children arrived the next day, nobody had told me many would be black. I was from a small village in Cheshire! I had been at Reading College and my last teaching practice was at Sunningdale, near Ascot!

It was very difficult for the children. They were from separate secondary schools: Morley, Sycamore and Huntingdon. There was great rivalry because of their loyalty to their schools.

I took needlework - very difficult. The kids were not too keen! As a naive teacher, I kept finding that needles were disappearing, only to find that the girls were using them to pierce their ears and then threading cotton through to keep the holes open.

I then became interested in Special Needs under the guidance of Chris Mills. She really taught me all I know now. I took 2H. Streaming existed in those days. Chris Mills retired from Elliott Durham a couple of years ago but last time I was up at E.D. she was still teaching as I think she had been recalled.

I began to organise dances for the older children. We had live black bands and some fabulous gigs.

We had an enthusiastic staff so we had a great social life. Our caretaker was Mr. Laing: great bloke. I taught Kirkland who went on to be a boxer. His Dad used to worry about him.

I had people to look up to: Mr. Oswell, Deputy Head. The children were in awe of him. But he was wise and always had time to talk to children who were sent to him. Miss Shaw, Deputy Headteacher, was a real lady and, again, the girls had great respect for her.

I loved every minute of my time at Elliott Durham. They were exciting times being in a new school. I left in 1971 to have my first baby. I was so sad!

****

Elliott Durham Head Teachers

J. Wyndham Davies 1966-78

Peter Bratton 1978-84

Robert Bailey 1984-91

Kathy Yates 1991 -

Notts Education Department archives

The Equerry-in-Waiting to The Duke of Edinburgh is desired by His Royal Highness to invite

Mr J. W. Davies

to attend the presentation of Awards to young people who have reached the Gold Standard in His Royal Highness's Award Scheme

at Buckingham Palace on Tuesday 25th March 1980

Dress: Lounge Suit or Uniform, Afternoon Dress

I WILL ALWAYS REMEMBER MY FIRST MORNING, says Tony Cerabona ('Antonio' at school). He is now 41 years old, married with two teenage children, and employed as a Customer Service Manager at Bristol Street Sherwood, one of Citroen's main dealerships in the Midlands.

I think myself very lucky and privileged to have attended the Elliott Durham Secondary Bilateral School in its opening debut in 1966 after moving up from Huntingdon Street Junior School. The massive demolition plan of the old St Anns area was taking effect in phases and necessitated several local schools in the area to close.

This was a very difficult period for all our family as we had been living in the area for over 14 years. Mum and Dad owned the house at 40, Dane Street, off Alfred Street Central. They had worked very hard and made many financial sacrifices to achieve this. It was very disconcerting that our home was being taken away and demolished.

I will always remember my first morning at a brand new school. I and many others travelled by local bus, but many walked to school. Hundreds of excited pupils bustled and pushed, slowly congregating in the huge playground. Everyone was confused with excitement and anticipation.

We were all immaculately dressed in our brand new uniforms. Even though some of the blazers were either too large or too small, all displayed proudly the prominent original red Maple Leaf badge, as the School was named after Canadian born Alderman Elliott Durham.

It was quite clear to me that due to the sheer size of the School premises and grounds, there was going to be a huge number of pupils attending this school. I think the school was receiving pupils from about five or six feeder schools.

The magnificent sports facilities available made it obvious that competitive sports activities were going to be very high in the School's physical education programme.

Approximately six hundred pupils slowly shuffled their way along the main foyer to congregate in the main assembly hall to be welcomed on stage by a silver-haired warm friendly faced Mr.J.W.Davies, the Headmaster, dressed in his black gown, together with all the other members of staff seated on the stage and adjacent balcony.

The School had six Houses which all the pupils individually represented when competing in sporting and academic competitions. The School also had an excellent gymnasium and swimming pool which were regularly used by the School and many other sporting bodies in the Nottingham area at County level competitions.

My younger brother, Giuseppe, joined the School two years later along with other friends and relations from the area. I experienced five very enjoyable years at the School, and represented it in many sporting teams.

We moved house in my final year after deciding to stay on in the 5th Year to take C.S.E's. I obtained seven C.S.E. passes, and one 'O' Level pass in Italian.

I then went on to a full apprenticeship in Motor Vehicle Technology, attending several local technical colleges.

I often meet many old school friends and teachers visiting our dealership at work, where we talk vividly of the nostalgic good old school days. I was personally involved in the successful 25th Anniversary School Reunion.

****

Hundreds of pounds were raised for the British Heart Foundation by pupils, teachers and ancilliary staff during a one-hour sponsored skip. As it turned out, the day was sizzling hot. From l to r are Leslie Gascoigne, school caretaker; Lynne Fielding, Librarian; Joanne Bull (12), pupil; Marian Donaldson, secretary; Kathy Yates, Deputy Head, and Robert Bailey, Headmaster

Nottingham Evening Post photo archive 22.6.89

THE BOYS MADE CHRISTMAS CAKES.

Dorothy Wroughton worked for four years as School Secretary at the Sycamore Girls' School. When it was amalgamated into the new Elliott Durham School in 1966, she was asked by the appointed Headmaster, Mr.J.W.Davies, if she would take on the job of Senior Secretary working 39 hours a week. Another Secretary was also appointed, for 29 hours 40 minutes per week. Dorothy Wroughton retired in November 1982. She writes:

I went into the new school in the Summer holidays of 1966 to put together the class lists and organise other work that had to be done before the school opened. All this was done working along with the Headmaster and the two Deputy Head Teachers.

The opening day was somewhat awe inspiring as there were approximately 1,000 pupils.

The school dinner system seemed daunting as there were so many wanting to stay for dinner. Many of them were on free meals as the St Anns area at that time was one of the deprived areas of Nottingham. We managed to arrange the dinners eventually but we had to have two or three sittings.

Once the House system was organised we were able to put the children into six Houses. Eventually the number of children who paid for their dinner dwindled, some of them going for chip butties from the local Fish and Chip shop, and one sitting became sufficient.

The six Houses were named after Canadian towns as Alderman Elliott Durham (after whom the School was named) was a Canadian. The Houses were:

EDMONTON, HUDSON, LAWRENCE, OTTAWA, TORONTO, VANCOUVER.

A few years after we opened, most of the old houses in St Anns were pulled down and new ones were later built. Meanwhile the families were rehoused elsewhere in the city and our numbers rapidly reduced. Eventually some families came back. But many of the new houses were two-bedroomed houses, so the larger families could not return. Numbers on the roll dwindled quite spectacularly. By the time I retired in 1982, they were below 500 pupils.

The School building had quite a few problems to start with, such as plate glass windows down to the floor level on the stair bends. We insisted that wooden bars were placed on the windows. Some windows were also unusable as they were obstructed from opening by concrete posts.

The School was very pleasantly set with playing fields around and several tennis courts. The Elliott Durham swimimng baths were situated at the top end of the School drive.

Inside the main building of the School were three floors. The ground floor was taken up with an entrance foyer with the Office and the Headmaster's Office incorporated. Along the corridors were the two Deputy Heads' offices, the staffroom, the Library, the Head Caretaker's Office, the staff tearoom, the Woodwork room and the Metalwork room.

The other floors were general class rooms, the Domestic Science and Needlework rooms being on the top floor. We also had our Main Hall and annexe approached by stairs going down from the foyer.

Apart from the main building, there was another building on the campus with two floors which housed the six dining rooms for pupils plus several more class rooms.

The Office equipment consisted of a telephone switchboard, which had extensions to all floors and both buildings, three typewriters and a duplicating machine. Eventually, the duplicator was moved to a room on the ground floor where a Reprographic Department was set up. Eventually, more reproducing equipment was obtained and a lady, who we trained in the Office, worked in this Department.

The pupils were of mixed race and, at one time during my time there, the percentage of ethnic minorities was 38%. In the early years, we had quite good GCE 'O' Level results but these tended to decline over the years.

Pupils from the Third Year and upwards had a timetable which included the boys having a term doing one or two periods a week of Domestic Science and the girls doing Metalwork or Woodwork. This brought out some very good results. The girls were very good, sometimes better than the boys, at woodwork. They made coffee tables, fruit bowls and smaller items. The boys were very good at making Christmas cakes. I can remember these well as they were on display for each class, in turn, to go and see. The girls' Woodwork was on display at the same time.

During the first few years, the older pupils were allowed a DISCO every Friday lunch time. This was quite successful, but I am sure some of them would be deaf by the time they were much older. It certainly had a deafening reaction on me as the Hall was just underneath the Office! Still, we didn't complain. It brought in a steady amount of cash for School Funds.

As a Senior Secretary, for most of my time I dealt with controlling the capitation, and also dealing with the School Fund monies. The other Secretary dealt with the dinner situation and monies. We both shared the typing, although most of mine was for the Headmaster. We both shared answering the switchboard.

After the first Headmaster, Mr.J.W.Davies, retired in 1978, Mr.P.Bratton was appointed. Soon after I retired, he took a post in Hove, near Brighton. As with Mr.Davies, Mr.Bratton and I worked very well together. Mr.Bratton passed the job of capitation to a member of staff to relieve me of my heavy load.

Capitation was the allocation of funds the Education Authority allowed to each school based on an amount per pupil. This was issued annually. My job (once the Headmaster had allocated an amount to each Department) was to check invoices as they came in and also to check that everything on the invoice had been delivered before sending the invoice to the Education Department. Also to make sure we spent all our capitation allowances otherwise we were given less the next year. This was quite a time consuming job as parcels were arriving once or twice daily.

Retirement get together. In the foreground, Head Secretary Dorothy Wroughton and husband, Stan. Middle (l to r) Miss K.Shaw, Eileen Cooper, Rick Stimson, Mr.J. W.Davies (sitting), Mr.A.Oswell. Derek Kirk standing at back

Individual's archive

Monies were raised for the School Fund by various activities, like the Friday DISCO already mentioned. I had the job of counting the money and banking it. I did the bookkeeping for these funds, which were used for non-curricular activities such as help for deprived children to have a holiday with a school party in Wales or Scotland etc.

We also held a party at Christmas for senior citizens at which most of the older children either entertained or they looked after the elderly people, such as helping them down the stairs to the Main Hall or serving them at table. This event was always a great success.

By the way, the sports teams were very good.

1st Year Choir 1979 *Elliott Durham photo*

I NEVER REALLY SHONE IN ANYTHING, says Jean Taylor (nee Morley) of her school days. After many years' varied and relevant practical experience she is now Warden of a complex for elders in Mapperley.

When the School opened, I lived on Norland Road off St Anns Well Road. Sycamore Girls' School closed down, and hundreds of teenagers from all areas moved to Elliot Durham. It was so big.

There was so much going on: outings, games, holidays. My class went to Devon. I had to drop out due to illness and another girl took my place. I was the only member of my family to attend this school.

With the houses being pulled down, we moved to Sherwood and I didn't stay on at school. I decided I would leave for work. That's 30 years ago. It's funny because I live in Mapperley now and pass the School often.

Mr. J. Bradshaw was my teacher (also Mr. J.M.Bain). He moved abroad. There was Mrs. C. Smith; Mr. Nehra and Miss S. Nehra (they were brother and sister) and Miss K.M.Shaw, Headmistress. When we changed for lessons in another part of the building, there were always lots of stairs to climb. I never really shone in anything and I wasn't a great speller.

But I remember the sewing teacher Miss Rougeault. I made a pair of frilled pillow cases (1966). The needle went through my thumb and I ended up going to the General Hospital to have it removed.

An entry in Jean's autograph book

Best wishes for the future. Don't wear your skirt too short!! J. Rougeault

When a teacher said JUMP, you always did as you were told. They were the most important part of the School: without their knowledge you wouldn't learn anything. So you always looked up to them. Looking back, some of them were very bossy and would pick on pupils for nothing.

It was the same with teenagers. Some were very cheeky (I often had the last say!). But I knew my place. From the road I lived on, the following crowd walked to school together: Jean Morley (me), Sandra and David Ashton, June Lowe, Rosa Belmonta, Steven Cranfield. Three friends called for me: Pauline Fedoriwskyi, Linda Bamford and Janet Watson.

When I left School, I worked at Farmers at the top of Exchange Walk. I was on the Soft Furnishings. My wage was £4.4s for a 40 hour week.

Out of the shop's top windows, I watched the Queen come to the Council house in 1967. Each Department had its own fresh smell and at the very top was the staff canteen. Two lovely ladies, both called Edna, did the cooking.

I spent a year in Minsons Factory (net curtains) in the Lace Market. I married in 1971 and worked part-time at the Co-op as a shop assistant. I had my daughter, Clair, in 1973, and am so proud she is a Staff Nurse.

I moved to Yarmouth in 1975 and back to Nottingham, 1977. In 1978, I became a Home Help Care Assistant but left after one year and saw the other side of life in a cosmetic surgery. In 1980, I went back to being a carer.

After ten years, I became a Warden at Beeston and, in 1993, came to Mapperley to run a complex on my own for Gedling Borough Council. I've always got on well with elders so I love the job and I used to say (if I was clever enough) I could write a book on things that have happened and stories that have been told to me.

Memories of when I was young, and living off St Anns Well Road, in poems was always my pastime. I'm trying to sort all my bits out and do a small book* at Office World before November when St Anns Library are doing an Open Day.

*Jean Taylor has written *Memories of St Anns Well Road, Nottingham*, which includes photos and her poems of times gone by. Available from St Anns Library [Ed].

Jean Taylor (far left) in photo taken at a reunion celebration, held at the School. The occasion raised £350 for the School's minibus appeal

Right, former students (from left) Cebert Dennis, Vivian Oliver (Head Boy in 1967) and Jestina Edwards present a cheque to pupil observers on the School's governing body, Emile Thomas and Nicola Pieretto.

Photos Nottingham Evening Post photo archive, 29.12.89 & 7.2.90

ELLIOTT DURHAM SCHOOL

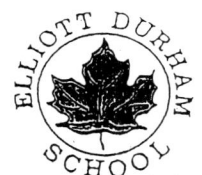

CLASSES OF 1966-1986

You are invited to

25th Anniversary Reunion

To be held at

ELLIOTT DURHAM SCHOOL

on

Saturday 13th July 1991

Admission £4.00

Including Raffle and Disco

Doors open 7.00 pm

Some ex-students recall the reunion photographed in the local Press on 29.12.89 as the 25th Anniversary Reunion, but the dates do not quite add up and there is the leaflet reproduced here and other written material which focuses on 1991 (which was 25 years after opening). Was there a reunion in 1989 **and** 1991?

****

Hudson House Prefects
1972-73

Elliott Durham photo

"There is so much going on here, we want to show the full range of work and leisure activities," said Head Teacher, Peter Bratton, as staff and pupils prepare a Day in the Life of Elliott Durham event for parents from five 'feeder' Primary Schools. Parents, he said, need not worry too much about the cost as specialist equipment was provided by the school. November 1983

Nottingham Evening Post photo archive

Three undated Elliott Durham photos which tell their own story about changes in technology: from the typewriter to successive generations of computers. The last photo appears in the current school brochure

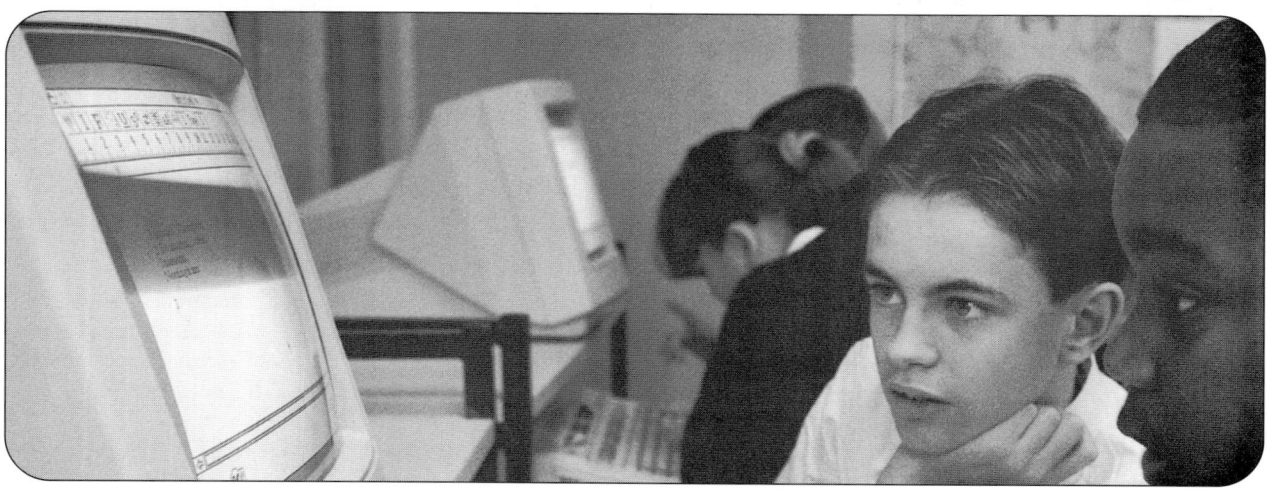

THE OFFSET LITHO KNOCKED SPOTS OFF THE BANDA,

said Janet K.Saunders, Resources Technician and Clerical Assistant 1970-1995, in her verse RETIREMENT PAPER produced below. She offered this to an appreciative audience at her farewell party, attended by many 'past hierarchy' including Mr.Wyn Davies, Mr.Arthur Oswell and Miss Kathleen Shaw. And Kathy Yates, current Head Teacher.

For my part, I was extremely sorry to be compelled to leave . . . age having caught up with me and I had already stayed the full course. So I planned to spend my savings on a one month holiday to Australia where I had a ageing aunt. This helped to soften the awful loss to me of 'my' school. The 'poem' describes something of the changes over the years as seen through the eyes of someone who was a sort of 'backroom girl.'

A RETIREMENT PAPER

I first set foot upon these grounds
    in 1953.
Some abandoned army huts stood here
    and one was given to me.

My homeless little family
    now had a roof to call our own
till we moved into a council house
    far beyond the town.

The years went by and I doubled my score
    of husbands and children, all daughters (four).
We lived locally then and by fate's cruel quirk
    the loss of my husband meant I had to work.

I was forty that year and to say life began
    is not quite the phrase I would pick.
I had so much to learn, some money to earn
    and a whole lot of problems to lick.

I followed advice and, to my joy found,
    a school had been built on the army camp ground.
It suited me then to start work at E.D.
    and it's suited me many long years you'll agree.

Elliott Durham has been for me
    a pleasure - a bit of a caper.
25 years of challenge and interest,
    of friendship - but most of all PAPER.

Paper in sheets, paper in packets,
    paper in reams delivered from Hacketts.
Paper to collate - to count and fold and staple,
    paper into booklets with a designer Maple.

The colour range in early days
      was much less comprehensive.
Today there is a wider choice
      from pastel to intensive.

Gone the quarto and foolscap
      and the wax and thermal skins.
Gone the duplicating carbons
      and the Banda spirit tins.

The sizes now are A's and B's.
      We've got used to the change:
That's what school is all about -
      rearrange and rearrange.

For years I roomed on B Floor
      but it was too far away
from the Library resources
      so they moved me down to A.

Grey steel shelving, known as 'Dexion'
      lined the workroom built by 'Tone.'
Angle iron, chipboard benches
      painted white for me alone.

Now, as I'm about to leave
      'Tone' has quite transformed the place.
Cupboard units, post formed worktops
      lots of sockets, lifts its face.

I've always liked machines and so
      I cast my mind to long ago.
Olivetti and Remington were the thing
      and Royal and Imperial reigned as king.

Printing machines have strewn my path
      from early Gestetner to Risograph.
Roneo, Philips, Xerox, and more Cannons
      than in the 1812 score.

The Electro Scanner was a nine day wonder
      while the Offset Litho knocked spots off the Banda.
That made one feel like an organ grinder
      churning out papers as you turned the winder.

The latest thing is the O.M.R.*
      and I hope it will be found
to be better than the OCCI**
      which never got off the ground.

*Optical Mark Reader
**Optical Coincidence Card Index

Radio prgrammes I once would record
        and dozens of sets of slides I stored
for staff to show on the slide projector
        but they went the way of the antique collector.

Reel to reel taping was given a go,
        we had Grundig, Ferguson, JVC and Sanyo.
Betamax came to augment the T.V.:
        the job of recordings was given to me.

VHS won the day, Betamax was redundant
        and then we had break-ins and lost our equipment.
After several of these, the windows were barred
        but life behind bars wasn't terribly hard.

At times, I felt like a 'Tweeny'
        that's an 'in-between' maid you know,
'cos I always seemed to be running
        from the office to that room below.

I was always just an 'Indian' -
        never quite a 'Chief.'
I didn't know the cost of things
        it wasn't then my brief.

But declining staff soon meant that I
        must choose and order what to buy.
And all must be accounted for
        so to my list of chores
were columns and columns of figures
        for me to draw half-termly scores.

Tasks in the Office took many forms
        apart from making tea.
Dinner Forms and Letting Forms and
        Uniforms: that's three.

The phone, the medicals, the Admissions Book
        the Registers covered each year.
The Inventr'y lists, the Copycard lists,
        the Christmas card lists: all here.

Retirement, I thought, was a millstone
        inevitable as doom:
always put off to the future,
        always regarded with gloom.

But retirement may not be the millstone
        I once thought it was,
since I decided to splash my savings
        on a trip of a lifetime to OZ.

So I'm going to substitute L for E
        and turn the mill into mile
and travel as far as funds will allow
        and pass the milestone with a smile.

The young lady taking over
        is a different sort of coin.
But she's learnt so very quickly
        that you'll scarcely see the join.

So it's time to say goodbye now
        I will try to keep my cool
as I thank you for the memories
        of my happy days at school.

Janet Saunders' two younger daughters attended Elliott Durham, after attending Walter Halls Junior School. Janet says the youngest, Rachel, was probably the first to take her French 'O' Levels six months early under the excellent tutelage of Annette Duflot, plus the good fortune in being able to send her for several trips to France. She obtained 8 'O' Levels and went to Bilborough Sixth Form College and then to Middlesex Polytechnic to take a four year course in European Business Studies. Two of the years were spent in Rheims. She gained a BA Hons degree in 1984 and went on to become a Marketing Manager. Now married, she has two children.

Janet's second daughter who went to Elliott Durham did things the other way round. After several jobs (the best as a dental assistant: a direct result of the Work Experience Week she was given at school), marrying 11 years ago with children now 8 and 10, she has become a mature student on a three year degree course. She aims to become a teacher.

"I have always felt that Elliott Durham deserved a better reputation than it acquired," comments Janet.

School secretaries Janet Saunders and Linda Miller give a lift on their broomsticks to an American footballer, alias teacher Robin Tinker

They are raising £450, together with other staff and pupils, for hurricane stricken Jamaica and flood victims in Bangladesh

Individual's archive, undated

Nottingham Evening Post

Jamaica Information Service says Hurricane Gilbert struck 12.9.88

NEW CHALLENGES.

Matthew Ward did his Third Year Undergraduate Thesis as part of his BA Degree in History/Politics at the University of Newcastle upon Tyne (March 1994) on Parental Choice and the Elliott Durham.

His Thesis spells out some of the current challenges for Elliott Durham, and schools with similar locations in the UK. The 72-page Thesis offers background and analysis of the implications, practice and results of the way in which current parental choice operates. The following extracts are selected as they assist in recording Elliott Durham's history.

Matthew Ward was a student at Elliott Durham 1983-88. He is now a Primary School teacher in Newcastle upon Tyne. He is far right on the bottom row of the photo below. It was taken during his first year at Elliott Durham.

The names of students in this photo are fortunately attached to it. Top row (l to r) are Julia Williams, Josephine Mayes, Ann Marie Sylvester, Deborah Kirk, Julie Raven, Charlotte Bowler, Monica Moran, Caroline White. Middle row (l to r) are Karen Crofts, Jason Newton, Brian Pearson, Ian Scott, Mark Reeves, Dawn Hayes, Deborah Briggs, Karen Bryce, Misbah Majid. Bottom row (l to r) are Lloyd Robinson, Philip Purcell, Paul Margeson, John Grieg, Dean Joseph, Mohammed Gaffur, Matthew Ward   *Elliott Durham photo*

Background of recent educational Politics

Both the Right and the Left acknowledge that the 'open enrolment' constituent of the 1988 Education Reform Act was a major step towards the opening up of schooling to the 'Market.' Education is becoming a product to be chosen by 'consumers' - parents - just like toothpastes, soft drinks and cars. People choose their cars for a variety of reasons including appearance, cost, prestige value, safety, and marketing as well as efficiency and performance. The ability to choose wisely and then be able to exercise that choice depends on, amongst other things, wealth, knowledge of cars and the ability to assess one's own needs. Yet too often it is flashy packaging, catchphrases and subtle advertising that convince consumers to buy rather than the latter motives . . . According to the Right, the free flow of information and the opening of enrolment to all schools decreases the advantages of the wealthy and presents all parents with the chance to pick the school best suited to the needs of their child . . .

When I arrived at the Elliott Durham in 1983 there were over 800 pupils at the school. Now my younger brother has only 470 fellow pupils. For a number of years I wondered what caused such a major fall in the School's rolls . . .

The bulk of my information was gathered through face to face interviews . . . Mr. J.W.Davies gave colour to my picture of the School's history. As the first Head (1966-78) he was able to provide a fascinating and amusing description of the founding of the School and its infancy. The history of the School was continued by Roger Tanner (teacher at Elliott Durham 1978-83, now Deputy Head of the nearby Frank Wheldon Comprehesive) who also offered useful comparisons between 'the Elliott' and the Frank Wheldon. My knowledge of the School was brought up to date by the present Head, Kathy Yates . . .

I received a great deal of help from Notts Local Education Authority, especially Mick Jones (Assistant Director Development) who furnished me with county-wide facts and figures; and Peter Housden, the Director of Education . . . Alan Simpson MP provided a broader picture of the problems of St Anns with some inspiring suggestions for the future of the School . . .

Over the twenty-seven years since the School was opened the education system of England and Wales has been subject to a series of major upheavals, firstly moving to the Left and then decisively Rightwards . . .

The Education Act of 1980 introduced a number of measures claimed to enhance parents' choice. Chief of these were new rights of parents to choose their child's school and the Assisted Places Scheme in which the State paid for able children to go to Private Schools.
. . . In the short term parental choice was sacrificed to efficiency and cost cutting. The Goverment realised that local authority management of education provision was the least expensive alternative at a time of falling rolls and massive cutbacks in public expenditure. The Act enabled parents to demand a certain school for their child unless compliance with the preference would 'prejudice the provision of efficient education or the efficient use of resources.'

Therefore, although knowledgeable parents, increasingly, could have their child educated out of the catchment [area], the Local Education Authorities still had the power to regulate admission, primarily by fixing artificial ceilings of up to 20% on popular schools' intake. Peter Housden, the Director of Education for Nottinghamshire, claimed that in the years following the Act "fewer than one per cent" of parents lodged an appeal in that county . . .

Under the provision of the 1988 Act parents were given unrestricted access to the school of their choice until that school has reached its physical capacity as defined by the 1979 standard number . . .

The National Curriculum is part of a whole package which makes up the 1988 Educational Reform Act. Its enforced testing and assessment requirements are part of the method in which the Government hopes to classify schools in order to facilitate parental choice. These published results are heralded as 'performance indicators' of a school . . .

The Whitepaper 'Choice and Diversity' [1992] and the subsequent Act of 1993 strengthened the legislation of 1980, 1986 and 1988 which forced schools to make public such information as exam results. In 1994, there are nationally published league tables showing the exam results and truancy rates of all State schools . . .

The Whitepaper of 1992 stated that "where a school is failing pupil numbers will fall . . . the school will not be able to achieve the high educational standards desired for all pupils." It goes on to say . . . "it is wrong to allow this to happen . . . the solution is to remove surplus places and close surplus schools" . . . Therefore, if parents choose not to send their children to a certain school, that 'failing' school, as already asserted, must be a bad one and will have to improve or perish.

What happens to the 'choice' of the parent who wants his or her child to attend the Wilford Meadows school but through the decision of a minority of local parents to look elsewhere find that their choice has been removed as the local school has been closed down?

In 1987 Tim Brighouse, the then Chief Education Officer for Oxfordshire, outlined his fears for parental choice and educational provision in the county if 1988 introduced 'open enrolment.'

He described the situation in the town of Witney which had two Comprehensives, one an ex-Grammar school and the other a former Secondary Modern. Despite similar academic success rates the ex-Grammar school was far more popular amongst parents than its neighbour. Brighouse claimed that if it were not for the powers of the Local Education Authority to control numbers at each school one would go to the wall. " . . . one of these perfectly good schools might have been crippled by innuendo and rumour . . . and the other would have been painfully overcrowded" (Article in The Independent, 1987). The free extent of 'open enrolment' would leave parents with greatly diminished, if any, choice and the growing town would be represented by only one school.

****

Elliott Durham 1966-1994

In 1994 with a roll one-third of the official capacity, exam results situating the School in the county's bottom half dozen and a truancy rate of 7% half days missed in 1993, the School appears to fit the Right's criteria of a failing school. A brief history of the Elliott Durham gives a better understanding of the apparently grim statistics above. One of the fundamental reasons for not choosing a school is its reputation. Studies show how these reputations can prejudice opinions on schools for years to come . . .

In 1966 Nottinghamshire LEA decided to close down St Anns' three secondary modern schools and transfer the pupils to a brand new school built on extensive land which had formerly been a rifle range and allotments. The amalgamation of Huntingdon, Morley and Sycamore Girls' produced a first day roll of 869 pupils and 48 staff. The School had bilateral status which meant it was devoid of the top 25% of pupils, who went to grammar school, but was expected to raise the expectations of its top 20% to go on to one of the new sixth form colleges.

Consequently, a substantial number of pupils - especially girls - who had not been entered for examination at their old schools found increased opportunity in the new School. "I believe we realised the potential of many more children" (J.W.Davies, Head 1966-78). The situation of the School offered great possibilities yet also grave problems.

Although built in the white skilled working class suburb of Mapperley, it drew most of its pupils from the deprived St Anns, half a mile down the hill. Consquently in an area where there had only been the Walter Halls Primary School there were soon approximately a thousand kids coming in every day.

The local community hardly welcomed the School with open arms: "Many saw it as an invasion" (J.W.Davies). There were predictable complaints from local shopkeepers, but more worrying disdain from the chief community figures. The Headmaster, Davies, called a meeting of the local community in June 1967 to try and establish links and elicit support. He was "bitterly disappointed" by both the low turnout and the lukewarm reponse. According to Davies, the local church, St Judes, was only 75% committed to the school, indeed the lacklustre reception afforded its pupils at a school carol concert* prompted the enraged Head to sever links and look elsewhere for future venues.

During these early years the residents of the affluent Mapperley Park found a number of new visitors alongside the foxes and sqirrels in their gardens. One irate woman rang the School to complain of numerous Elliott Durham pupils 'scrumping' her apples. She snapped: "If only they had asked I would have given them some." The following day, a stern Head lectured in assembly against trespassing and repeated what the woman had said. Around lunchtime, he received another angry 'phone call, this time from the woman's husband who demanded to know who had told the pupils they could have free apples. He complained that all through dinner a queue of some forty-two children had asked for apples. The lighthearted story has a serious edge. Large sections of the local community, fearful of the 'rough' working class St Anns kids, and especially black children, turned their backs on the School and have had little to do with it ever since . . .

The School suffered in terms of reputation and organisation and a number of factors out of its hands. The influx of immigrants, mainly from the Indian sub-continent, created a number of challenges. School rolls could suddenly increase. For example, in September 1966 there were 869 pupils, but by January 1967 this had risen to 1,100, many of whom according to Davies arrived at the School with virtually no notice. Many children quite literally transferred over a weekend from a small village in Azad-Kashmir to the middle of Nottingham.

Problems were compounded by a Director of Education who believed children would pick up English without any extra assistance. "His attitude was let Davies get on with it (Davies)." It was only some years after the initial problem that much needed English as a Second Language provision was granted to the School.

In 1969, just as the School was settling down it went through a sudden and almost total upheaval as the slum clearance of St Anns got under way.

"It was crazy that they built the School and then the estate" (Roger Tanner, teacher at Elliott Durham 1978-83 and now Deputy Head of Frank Wheldon Comprehensive School).

The old community of St Anns was dismembered as all the old terraced houses were torn down. A large number of the original families were moved out and many new ones arrived.

---

* Mr.J.W.Davies says at the second carol service held at St Jude's Church, Mapperley, the school choir was not allowed to sing and there was recorded carol music. Thereafter, the school carol service was held at the Methodist Kings Hall, St Anns [Ed]

"The School's rolls concertinad . . . we never knew the situation day in or day out" (Davies).

The dislocation between School and catchment area compounded the distance already felt by parents as a result of the gap between the School and St Anns. The apparent chaos and the spotlight on the problems of St Anns enhanced the School's reputation amongst Mapperley parents. Several people suggested in interviews that it might have been better to build the School right in the middle of St Anns as a true community school (Roger Tanner) or at least closer to access roads (Alan Simpson MP, ex-Chairman of the Governors of the Elliott) . . .

The School turned Comprehensive in 1974/75. However over the last twenty years it has failed to attract a fully representative intake from the catchment area. In particular, parents in Mapperley Park and Mapperley turned elsewhere. Many Mapperley Park children went to private schools, some parents would move to other catchment areas when their child reached eleven and a number appealed to get their child into other schools, especially after 1980. A significant number of Mapperley children did attend the Elliott, the bulk of whom came from the adjacant Querneby Road area.

Roger Tanner was involved in community work at the School between 1978 - 83. He claims it attracted "only a dozen or so ex-grammar school type children." These came from the private housing estate of Penarth Gardens in Mapperley and made up the School's top class. Tanner complained that as a result of this, the School received little help from the local community, except from the Querneby area. Therefore, the focus of the School was more than ever in St Anns . . .

Although the majority of pupils come from St Anns, even parents there have begun to look to schools away from the area. As the area suffers social problems many parents do not want their child linked with the poverty of St Anns. In 1994, the Elliott Durham has to compete with schools in neighbouring catchments for pupils. It does not start from a level playing field in this fight.

Declining intakes

. . . "There are surplus places in Nottingham and you can't keep shoring up schools when running a tight budget" (Elliott Durham Head, Kathy Yates, in Nottingham Evening Post, October 1993).

In October 1993, the County Council announced a short list of ten secondary schools at risk of closure from which two would be selected. One of the ten was the Elliott Durham. A month earlier, Kathy Yates had forecast such developments and expressed her fears.

> " . . . the authority is fearful of being rate-capped for a second year running so is looking for ways of saving money in the education budget . . . they will 'reorganise' education in the area which means the closure of certain schools . . . we could be at risk. I hope not."
>
> (Interview 21st September 1993)

The School Accommodation in Nottinghamshire report of November 11th 1993 ended the anxious wait by proposing the Padstow and Wilford Meadows schools for closure. These schools had the second and third lowest occupancy rates in the City at 36.3% and 36.4% respectively in 1992/93. The Elliott with the fourth lowest, 40.2%, was reprieved.

Over all the secondary schools in Nottinghamshire the occupancy rate was 62.6% in 1992/93 which realised 8,000 surplus places. The surplus places were especially concentrated in the north of the city, where the Padstow is located, and in the south where both Wilford Meadows and the Elliott Durham are situated. One of the factors influencing the reorganisation is the expense of small schools. The budget share per pupil of the Wilford Meadows was £2,746.68 compared to the 1992/93 average of £1,971.23.

The report cites three main reasons for low occupancy rates in some city schools: demographic change, the Djanogly City Technology College, and 'open enrolment.'

During the 1980's the Elliott Durham's size declined dramatically, from around 900 in the early part of the decade to 470 in 1984. The question to be addressed is whether the fall in numbers is attributable to open enrolment, demographic shifts or other factors.

Demographic change

In common with nationwide trends, Nottinghamshire experienced a colossal fall in the number of school children during the 1980's. The fall in birthrate during the 1960's and 1970's, one-third in Notts, is the major cause of surplus places today. The education system which had expanded enormously on the crest of the baby boom, found itself with a residue of thousands of surplus places as numbers retracted.

Numbers in secondary education in the county fell from 87,303 in 1980/81 to a low of 62,042 in 1989. The city experienced an even more dramatic slump from 22,753 to 13,219. 1982 saw the lowest intake in the city's primary schools so, as expected, 1988/89 realised the least first formers enrolling at secondary schools. Numbers began rising slowly in the mid 1980's in primary schools and finally had an impact on secondary levels from 1991 onwards. According to the Local Education Authority's summary projections Nottingham's secondary school pupil numbers will rise from 13,501 in 1993/94 to 16,125 at the turn of the century. The occupancy rate of 62.6% in 1993/94 will rise to 78.4% in 2002/03. However, in the southern area of the city even an increase of 7% will leave 2,146 surplus places . . .

The Elliott Durham and other inner-city schools experienced the effects of demographic change far more than schools slightly farther out. Over the 1980's virtually no new council housing was built in the St Anns area. Although Housing Association development has gone some way to filling the gap, there have been fewer families settling in the area, and what new housing there has been tends to be far less dense than before. The rise In living standards for some and an increase in the numbers of owner occupiers has caused a drift away from the inner-city towards the suburbs. The move is fuelled by the real and exaggerated fears of drugs and crime, combined with a wish not to be associated with a stigmatised area for reasons of employment and social standing.

City Technology College

. . . The Government's announcement in 1986 of the plan to establish 20 city technology colleges was interpreted in many ways. The Government claimed they would be 'beacons of excellence', that would stimulate diversity and improve other inner city schools through their example . . .

. . . The Government failed badly in its attempts to make business carry most of the costs. Sponsors' contributions have fallen to around 20% whilst the rest of the money comes from public money.

Up to 1991 only in Bradford and Bermondsey schools had sponsors who paid more than 20% of costs . . .

. . . Djanogly City Technology College, Nottingham, takes 825 pupils out of the Local Education Authority maintained system and because of its limits all are from the city catchment area. The places available in one year are 165 and since its inception the school has consistently reached around this target, with a peak of 175 in 1992 . . .

. . . The City Technology College "has taken one whole class out of teaching" (Kathy Yates, Head of Elliott Durham).

The City Technology College attracted seventeen pupils from the Elliott Durham catchment area in 1993, some 9% of the total.

. . . Motivated pupils and parents that the City Technology College attracts are desperately needed by a school like the Elliott Durham to maintain the balance of the school toward learning and achievement. The school risks losing disproportionately high numbers from certain sectors of society to the College, especially those of a South Asian background . . .

. . . It is interesting to note the views of one set of Mapperley parents who sent their child to the City Technology College. Chief among their beliefs was concurrence with the school's publicity that children need to be able to fit the needs of industry. Interestingly the father had been amongst the first batch of pupils to transfer up to the Elliott Durham in 1966. He linked the excitement he felt at his own brand new school with the favourable impression given by the purpose-built modern City Technology College . . . .

'Open Enrolment'

. . . The demographic trough occurred in 1988/89 concerning numbers of eleven year olds and since then numbers in the catchment area have slowly risen to around 180. The major drop in numbers at the Elliott happened in the mid to late 1980's as small first forms replaced much larger departing fifth forms. However although these years have moved up through the school with larger numbers in the catchment area now available, the school's rolls have continued to decline.

The reason behind this is a change in the percentage in the catchment area sending their children to the school of some 20% since 1988. Before 1988, around 66% of eligible children attended the school but by 1993 this had fallen to 46%. Some 55% of children in the catchment area now went elsewhere.

So, despite the bulk of the numerical fall occurring before 1988, the drop since then has been greater than it appears as it has coincided with an increase in numbers in the catchment area. 'Open enrolment' seems to have had an enormous impact on removing up to 20% of the potential intake.

Rather than experiencing an increase due to the enlarged pool of children, the school has suffered a continued decline [in numbers], a fact with severe repercussions for the future ...

. . . Before 1988, some parents chose other schools for consistent reasons such as religion. Catholics who went to lay primary schools tended to go to the Catholic Beckett or Christ the King Comprehensives, a number of Muslim girls went to the all girl Manning School, and the Bluecoat Church of England School attracted a dozen or so pupils each year. The large numbers of Mapperley Park children who attended private schools at both primary and secondary level are not counted in the calculation of catchment area numbers. Only children in State feeder schools are numbered. A few pupils from the feeder schools took an entrance exam for the independent Nottingham High School but rarely more than a couple enrolled.

Since the school's inception, very few middle class parents had enrolled their offspring at the Elliott. Increasingly after 1980 these parents appealed to have their child go to other schools. Roger Tanner claims that aware parents quickly grasped the implications of the Great Debate which gradually diffused over the 1980's. In the lower middle class enclave of Alexandra Park only two out of fifteen children enrolled at the Elliott between 1980 and 1986 . . .

In 1993, the Arnold Hill Comprehensive, a mile north of the Elliott, attracted 127% of its catchment [numbers] and the Frank Wheldon Comprehensive School gained 94.8%. In the same year the Elliott Durham enrolled only 46% of the children from its feeder schools losing numbers to both these schools. Only 78 of a possible 171 transferred to the school, the other 93 being dispersed around the county's schools.

The chief gains were the City Technology College (17 pupils), Manvers (13), Manning (11), Frank Wheldon (8), Arnold Hill (8), Bluecoat (7) and Gedling Comprehensive (4). Individual pupils went to ten or more other schools. This indicates one of the problems for an inner-city school i.e. that parents have a myriad of options of other accessible schools.

Morley Junior School, a school right in the middle of St Anns and with direct road access to Elliott Durham, sent the highest percentage of pupils to the school, 64% in 1993 (24 pupils). Of those pupils who did not go to the Elliott Durham, the majority went to the all girl Manning school or the Church of England Bluecoat school. Next highest after the Morley Junior are the Sycamore and Elms schools who transfer around 50% (17 and 9 respectively). Both of these schools are also in the St Anns estate but slightly closer to the city and other schools. From these schools, most non-Elliott pupils went primarily to other inner-city schools. The majority of Elms pupils not transferring to the Elliott Durham in 1993 were Muslim girls who went to the all girl Manning, and from the Scyamore the bulk went to the nearby Manvers school, a Comprehensive with a similar reputation and even worse absolute exam results than the Elliott Durham.

None of the 60% from the Walter Halls who went to school out of the catchment area in 1993 enrolled at other city schools, excepting the City Technology College and the Bluecoat school. Walter Halls parents face outwards and use the easy access of the Woodborough Road to send their children to schools in all white estates with high rates of private housing, such as two schools in Arnold, the Redhill (3) and Arnold Hill (6), the Frank Wheldon (7) in Carlton and Gedling Comprehensive (1).

Only 30% of Huntingdon's pupils moved up to the Elliott Durham in 1993. This has a lot to do with the proximity of the school to the city centre. The equal accessibility of other schools than the Elliott Durham was reflected by the choice of eleven different schools for the junior school's 37 pupils. A number, as from all St Anns schools, went to secondary schools in other council estates due to moving house or family connections and 18% went to Manvers or Manning. However, 12 pupils (32%) went to the City Technology College, one more than to the Elliott. The locality of the school and the aspirations of many of the school's Asian parents may partly explain this high figure that accounts for all but five of the 17 pupils who went to the City Technology College from the Elliott's catchment area in 1993.

Parental choice

. . . Available evidence clearly demonstrates that contrary to the Government's claim, parents do not necessarily pick out schools which offer the best education. Parental choice of school is motivated by a complex process of reasoning with a heavy emphasis on the happiness of the child. Partly through a belief that their child will be happier and safer there, and equally because of higher overall exam results, parents' choice is heavily biased toward schools with pupils from higher socio-economic backgrounds. The desire to get their child away from the 'taint' of working class city areas is strong in many parents.

Exams are seen as a way up the social ladder and equally moving the child away from a poor city school is part of that process. **As a school's academic performance is usually judged by its unadjusted exam results and as these results on the whole merely reflect the school's socio-economic intake, a good school will be one in advantaged areas whilst those in poor districts run a disproportionate risk of being labelled poor despite little evidence of the effectiveness of either.**

If these factors are combined with the evidence that better off and better educated parents are more likely to exercise and obtain choice and therefore places in more popular schools, then increased social segregation is likely . . .

. . . It is obvious that 'open enrollment' presents the risk of a downwards circle as the proportion of able children falls so that the likelihood that less will enrol is increased. The 1992 Whitepaper 'Choice and Diversity' declares that one of the key conditions for success in schools is: "a high level of parental and community support."

> Kathy Yates pointed out one minor detail which causes considerable problems for the school, the fact that so many parents do not have telephones so if the school has problems with a child they have to take them home themselves, a cost of much needed time and manpower.

. . . The structure of our society is such that there has always been a gulf in attainment and class of intake between schools in disadvantaged areas and those in the leafy suburbs. However, since 1988 the inequalities have increased both in terms of numbers and types of pupils and material resources. The two tier system that is being consolidated in Nottingham is one of a large number of prosperous and oversubscribed suburban and rural schools compared to cash and pupil starved rump schools in disadvantaged estates, the inner cities and ex-mining areas. If the process of polarity continues so will the inequality of resources, staffing and numbers, and ability range of pupils.

Whereas Nottinghamshire, in common with many authorities, delegated disproportionately high funds to schools with disadvantaged intakes, this has been stripped down basically to extra finance due to the percentage of free school meals in a school. The impact of money lost to the Elliott is reflected in the transitional payments to the school of £72,000 p.a. at present. The effects on staffing have been severe. The disproportionately generous staffing to keep classes small has been drastically reduced. In 1993 the school was forced to cut back by 5.1 and, as a worrying precedent, several redundancies had to be made.

Another change to the detriment of the Elliott Durham and schools with many disadvantaged pupils is the removal of funding for 'extras' such as school trips. Schools with larger intake and more money and those with wealthier intakes are able to provide more 'extras.' The Elliott Durham, despite contributions from the tuckshop and FRED [Friends of Elliott Durham. Not now active. 1997], had to charge pupils 50% more for a camping trip in 1993 than in the previous year, a deterrent for many poorer pupils.

The extra costs for which schools can appeal to parents will mean that larger schools with wealthier pupils will be better resourced and therefore even more popular. What is more it raises the potential of poorer parents being unable to send their children to schools where they cannot afford these demands.

The Right's claim of 'equality of access' sounds hollow in a society where the higher the socio-economic group the greater the levels of education, awareness and ability to play the system . . .

Maybe in the case of the Elliott Durham, exam results play a far more decisive role in determining choice of school than the national research shows. To Walter Halls parents [the adjacent Junior school] the gap between the 11.9% GCSE passes between grades A-C at the Elliott Durham in 1993 and the 48.2% at the Arnold Hill or the 59.5% A-G grades at Elliott Durham compared with 85.3% at the Frank Wheldon must be clearly evident.

Bearing in mind the evidence that parents accept unadjusted exam results as a mark of success rather than the progress of children at the school, it seems obvious that confronted with such a difference in attaintment they will turn their backs on the local school . . .

> Kathy Yates said that the comments and actions
> of other parents are a major influence on people's
> choices of schools. "Intakes year to year often
> depend on the influence of parents in a school
> i.e. if one able child with strong parents goes to
> the Elliott Durham it often influences others to
> go there."

One parent who intended to send their child to the Elliott Durham complained that "the league tables are extremely damaging and very misleading as to the value of the school."...

John Patten (Secretary of State for Education) heralded league tables as part of the 'information revolution' which let parents 'call schools to account.'

However, many educationalists and parents are demanding information be published showing the actual progress of a child at a school rather than the league tables of results. Distinguished figures such as Sir Ron Dearing have joined the campaign for 'value added' tables including background and prior attainment to be set beside raw examination data. There are signs that Patten may be wavering in his opposition. In its Editorial on the league tables on November 26th 1993, The Guardian declared:

> **"By itself the raw material is meaningless:**
> **clever intakes produce clever results...crude**
> **tables not only punish highly successful schools**
> **in deprived areas, but also camourflage the**
> **failure of poor performance in affluent suburbs."**

Naturally the league tables recorded the highest results in suburbs and rural areas and the worst in inner-city areas.

"The league tables are an enforced and sickening parade of the poor and disadvantaged in rank and order behind the more prosperous schools of the leafy gin and tonic belt." Nigel de Gouchy, NASUWT quoted in The Guardian 17.11.93.

Quality of Teaching

One debatable question is whether the loss of aspiring parents affects the quality of teaching at the school. Does the lack of parental pressure and involvement in their child's education mean that the bad teacher can lurk unnoticed in the school? Roger Tanner claims that this is not the case at the Elliott Durham. On the contary: "To work with challenging kids the teacher needs to be better." He said many teachers of his generation want to teach at inner-city schools for ideological reasons.

Maybe there are some grounds for concern at schools like Elliott Durham if this is the case. What will happen when these teachers, who came into education in the Sixties and seventies, are replaced by the outcrop of the 1980's and 1990's, decades wrapped in entirely different ideological covers?

The Elliott Durham which serves one of the most deprived inner-city areas of Nottingham defended its results and called for the tables to be scrapped: "We are doing the same sort of work as any other school, but the different levels of ability and language have meant we don't do as well as the others . . ."

Alan Simpson MP claimed a testimony to the strength of teaching at the school was the number of staff who go on to senior posts in other schools.

It has been suggested that able children may even do better at the school. As the balance is skewed towards the less able, bright children usually go straight to the top class whereas in another school they might have been in a middle band and have less expected of them. There are a number of criticisms to be raised concerning this last statement. Not least that it discounts the importance of peer pressure in pushing a child to attain or equally in discouraging work and success.

The OFSTED report of March 1994 claims the school has low academic results but these are in keeping with levels of disadvantage amongst the intake. **Importantly it asserts that ALL teaching was satisfactory or above. The school was found to be caring and disciplined.**

An H.M.I. visit in 1993 shed some interesting light on the gulf between views held by parents about the school and its actual performance. The inspectors described the school as 'welcoming' . . . with a positive ethos . . . " One of the most rewarding statements from the report was that: "All children spoken to rallied round and supported the school. See it as a school which has improved and value it. Right spirit."

The future

. . . The immediate future of the Elliott Durham as an institution appears to be secure. If current trends persist then numbers should rise slightly over a decade. **One significant statistic is that only four of the pupils who enrolled at the school in 1993 did not pick the Elliott Durham as their first choice. This suggests a fairly stable base of parents who expect to send their children to this school.** The four were those waiting to receive places at the City Technology College: all enrolled there.

What can the school do for its pupils in the present society? "The Elliott Durham has to continue to give the kids a sense of self worth, enthusiasm and fun carved out of a sense of not having a lot" (Alan Simpson MP).

Alan Simpson said that he chose the Elliott for his children for a mixture of reasons, including ideological ones. However he said the ideological ones only stretched so far as there was a positive choice between inner-city schools. In the end he claimed that the Elliott Durham represented that positive choice as he was very impressed by the school.

Part of his choice was the belief that his children would gain lifestyles equally as important as exam results by going to the school . . . "they gained more than they lost . . . maybe there is a lack of academic push but they gain a sense of living, understanding and surviving life in the city."

****

Harvest Festival gifts, 1982   *Elliott Durham photo*

Elliott Durham photo

Two photos of the 1980's.
The one below is of the school staff in 1982. If you look at this book carefully, you will recognise some of the faces. But can anyone send us a chart of who they ALL are (surnames and first names/initials)?

Individual's archive

Andrew Scothern (16) was given a lift in a chauffeur driven civic car to school as a celebration for being the first student to have achieved a 100% attendance rate over five years. What happened? It was held up in traffic! With his dad and grandma on board, he arrived 20 minutes late, as Kathy Yates is showing him on the clock

*Nottingham Evening Post
10.5.97*

Work Experience

To help Year 11 students make their decisions, the school is currently organising for them to go out on their final work experience placement. Businesses throughout the city welcome our students in this project providing every one involved with a positive experience. If you are interested if finding out more about the programme or would like to offer a work placement to one of our students, please contact Pat Whitby at the school on Nottingham 9523838.

Where are they now?

City Challenge money has also helped our students make choices for when they leave school. Whilst they are at school they experience college visits, work placements and practice interviews.

When they leave most of the young people study for A levels or a GNVQ.

The school is well positioned for pupils to chose from a variety of colleges.

Of the students who carry on to Higher Education many come back to see us to tell us of their success at degree level or above.

Above, two items from CONTACT (see also page 64)

Kariann Barker (15) won £500 for the school in a 'design a cover' competition run by Nottinghamshire County Council. She was given a box of 72 Derwent pastel pencils. Kariann is seen here with Kathy Yates, Head Teacher, and Jeremy Prentice (from competition sponsors TSB). Her design was completed as part of her GCSE art course

*Nottingham Evening Post
9.2.96*

Nicky Brett, Abbotsford Drive, St Anns, won the School's Governors' Award which is presented to students who show outstanding personal endeavour. He reacted quickly when rough weather caused canoes to capsize during a canoeing lesson at Colwick Park Lake. When he knew five of his friends were in difficulties: "All I was worried about was getting them to safety." He pulled one to the nearest island and then ferried several from the island to the bank. Rob Bailey, Head Teacher, said all were wearing life-belts and safety equipment but that should not detract from the fact that Nicky showed great presence of mind and an unselfish attitude. "This incident sums up Nicky's personality more than a school report would ever do," he added   *Nottingham Evening Post photo archive*

A framed front page of the special Elliott Durham supplement (see also pages 6 and 66) produced by the Nottingham Evening Post being presented to Herman Bailey (far left) and Susan Mallot, both 14. They helped to prepare the supplement. The framed copy is being given by the TSB Mapperley Branch Manager, Frank Hastings. Robert Bailey, Head Teacher, is second left. 31.10.84   Nottingham Evening Post photo archive

Elliott Durham photo

AN EXPERIMENT IN LOCAL HISTORY.

This Chapter outlines some work done by Year 9 students when Ruth I.Johns led some sessions in classtime followed by voluntary lunchtime local history meetings (also see Introduction and pages 70-72).

It was good being back in Elliott Durham. When I arrived each week, after signing in at Reception, I usually had some spare time which was spent chatting to whoever was about. For example, a 14-year-old inquired what I was doing in school. She expressed keen interest in finding out about St Anns' history. Several weeks later, she sought me out to inquire what we were doing that week. I particularly enjoyed the encounter when a somewhat stroppy youth was asked to show me up to the fourth floor. He offered a deep sigh to the universe, then asked me coolly for my views on the National Curriculum. He was obviously not going to depart until he heard them and discussed them! He was very knowledgeable. The ethos of a school comes across during these chance discussions.

****

BAD REPUTATION OF ST ANNS.

The 23 students in the classtime sessions referred to the unfairness of this reputation and how much it affected the way in which people who lived in St Anns were viewed. This subject recurred many times over the weeks of the Local History sessions (also see page 70).

Had any of the students experienced events which might confirm the 'bad reputation' image? Two spoke of having their homes burgled. One spoke of walking past a threatening youth with a broken bottle in his hand but nothing had happened. One said her mother feared leaving her and her brother in on their own when she had to work nights, so asked a relative to come from 16 miles away to stop over. One said her dog had been attacked by a Dobermann dog and its owner didn't seem to mind. One had experienced a violent boyfriend, and snippets circulated about problems at home experienced by some young people known to students.

Were these problems worse than in other areas? General agreement that problems in St Anns were more discussed. In 'better' areas, problems like domestic violence were still there but 'silently behind closed doors.'

"THERE IS A LOT TO FIND OUT"

There was keen interest about local history. It was voiced, for example, by Komal Pala who wrote the following in a special commemorative issue of Chase Chat (Spring 1995): **"St Anns is a big mystery. My friend and I got involved [in the local history sessions] because we both live in St Anns.**

"We first looked at personal case studies of people who used to live in St Anns, then we got into a wider range of topics such as the shops that are still in St Anns, the facilities around, and a timeline about past and present.

"The timeline gave us detailed information. Our group has done a lot and we have a feeling that people should get more interested in St Anns as it is their local area and there is a lot to find out about it."

LOCAL PEOPLE. One of the most popular parts of the local history sessions were the photocopies Ruth brought in from the one time St Anns community newspaper, Chase Chat. It included profiles on local people. One which particularly caught students' imaginations was the one [October 1974] reproduced here: the profile of Doreen Smith.

Her life illustrated many things about St Anns' life at that time, including education and work and it touched International history [the Vietnam War].

This profile led to lots of discussion and questions. Doreen was a survivor and the history surrounding her held attention.

Students wanted to know what happened to Doreen. Very quickly, she almost seemed like one of the family.

[The response to the Chase Chat cuttings indicated the important role community newspapers can play in creating a sense of community and in recording people and events. Ed]

If you have St Anns recollections about work; school; unemployment; parenthood; leisure; birth, life or death; community life; places of worship; housing; clubs: some special experience . . . or simply your ideas about the place . . .

Please write them down (in any style) and send them to the address on the back cover of this book. They will help build up recorded local history for future generations.

Photos always welcome

PERSONALITY PARADE

Doreen Smith

Mrs. Doreen Smith is chairwoman of this year's St. Ann's Festival. A working mum, with two children to bring up - Brett and Donna - Doreen lives in Bakersfield now.

She was born in St Anns, Doreen Simmonds, in the "good old days". Her father retired from work when Doreen was only seven months old. There were two other children older than Doreen. To keep them mother took in washing and worked as an ironer in a long-john works on Ashforth Street. They flitted from Broad Oak Street to Sherwin St, to Robin Hood Chase, to Peas Hill Road and back to the old St Anns Valley.

By this time her father had died and mother re-married. She got on well with her step-dad. After an education at the old St Anns Board School and then after eleven at Morley Senior, Doreen wanted to be a teacher, but she started work in the same factory as her mum, at the age of 14.

Young Doreen is the errand girl at the time of rationing. It paid the long-john works to pay a pound a week to some slip of a girl to slip out and join the queues for the other workers. Queues for sausage and cakes and anything. "If I saw a queue I'd join it," and back to the works with Woolworth combs and "Evening in Paris" rouge.

She stayed at Ashforth St. until she was 18 and her wages had risen to 35/- a week. She had learnt to pack and do the accounts in the office; and iron and machine in the hosiery.

Then, typical of her later life, she took a drop in pay at 19 to be a student nurse at Coppice Hospital. Then she was an instructress for Gestetner in Manchester.

At home one week end to see her step-father, she met 'Tub' Smith. They got married and nine months later were in California. Tub was a staff sergeant in the United States Air Force. They lived in a trailer home half way between Los Angeles and San Francisco.

She liked America : cleaner and bigger than home. She liked the way people had to stand on their own feet - and they did. She liked the higher standard of living, but not the price to be paid! Most people having to work at two jobs. After six years in the States, 'Tub' was called to Vietnam. Doreen was ill and so poorly she returned to Crown Street in St. Ann's, Phase Seven...but with an American accent!

The native girl found herself treated as an outsider. Feeling like an immigrant, her friends became the other immigrants of the neighbourhood - Indians, West Indians and Pakistanis came to Doreen for advice, about baby etc. And so it was she met Margaret Behrman and Barbara Levick, then living on Gordon Road.

In 1973 she joined SAMPH and, last year, the St. Ann's Festival. It's not quite like the Daughters of the British Empire, but of one thing she's sure; if she has anything to do with it, next year's Festival will be bigger and better and will embrace every organisation in St. Ann's!

FAMILY AND SCHOOL LINKS

Students suggested it would be interesting to find out how many of them now at Elliott Durham had relatives who had attended the School, or had families who lived in the 'old' St Anns.

And how many of them had relatives in St Anns now: that is relatives other than those in the household in which they lived?

Could we do a survey, they asked? I asked Ian Johnson, who said he would be willing to co-operate with a small survey.

A short questionnaire was circulated to 37 students (11/12-years-olds), and collected at the end of tutor sessions. I was excited about this project because it would go some way toward testing my own belief, from experience in St Anns, that family networks are considerable.

Little consideration has been given by outside commentators on the 'new' St Anns to the sense of community that has developed. It would be a pity to have to wait for some future clearance to appreciate positive aspects of today's community!

Twenty-nine of the respondents live in St Anns and 8 live just outside the area.

Of these 8, 4 have relatives who are now living in St Anns. 3 of the 8 have one set of grandparents and one a mother who lived in the 'old' St Anns before demolition. And 6 of the 8 have relatives who attended Elliott Durham. As well as siblings, these relatives include 3 parents, several aunts, one uncle and several cousins.

Of the 29 students who live in St Anns now, in addition to the family in the household in which they live, 16 have other relatives now living in St Anns.

These include one or more grandparents (in 6 instances), aunts, uncles, cousins and (separated) parents. A couple of the questionnaires were not fully completed, so possibly some more information was missed.

Twenty-one of the 29 have relatives who attended Elliott Durham, 15 having relatives other than brothers and sisters who did.

These other relatives included parents, aunts, uncles and cousins. Families with second generation attachment to Elliott Durham include longstanding local families who returned to the 'new' St Anns and those who came to the area when, or after, it was redeveloped.

This 'snapshot' of links between present students at Elliott Durham and St Anns shows that the School plays a considerable role as a continuing influence in the lives of local families and their community. It would be interesting if this study could be developed.

LUNCHTIME CLUB. Of the 6 students who attended the lunchtime local history group, 5 lived in St Anns. They had a variety of special interests. For example, the one who didn't live in St Anns went to the Sycamore Road Youth and Community Centre. Two played in the School Band which practises at the Springboard Social and Sports Centre for those with handicaps, one went to the Pakistan Centre and the Jipac Community project. One took her dog for a long walk before School each day. One did a daily work-out for an hour.

After one discussion about local amenities, several students wrote to Colin Haynes, of a Sneinton Community group called Bright Sparks, to support its proposed Sneinton/St Anns Playways scheme: a well thought out continuous cycle/pedestrian route linking small recreation grounds from Colwick Park to Robin Hood Chase at the top of St Anns. Colin came in one lunchtime to answer questions about the Project. What will happen to this locally researched and initiated proposal?

Students did considerable local history voluntary homework. For example, Claire Rogers interviewed her grandmother and mother. Her interview, on larger paper than that reproduced here, was illustrated with coloured sketches. See page 70 for more about the local history sessions

ST'ann's. by Claire Rogers.

Years ago my grandma says St Ann's was very different from today. She told me that none of the houses had indoor toilets or bathrooms. My nan and lots of other women took their washing on prams to the Victoria Baths, where, for a few pence they could fill a large sink with hot water and do the washing, and used huge driers. This took all day, usually a monday. Next door, people could have a bath, and you would pay for it, because it was so difficult at home with no hot water. My mum came to Nottingham in 1961 and her house in St Ann's had no indoor toilet or bathroom. My nan had to fill a metal bath in front of the fire to wash the children in. And to go to the toilet they had to put on a coat and shoes and run to the end of the yard to a little brick shed. There was a sink in the kitchen made of stone, and one tap with cold water.

St Ann's well Rd, still had trolley buses they were like trams and ran on tracks, The power came from a cable up in the air on poles that the trolleys looked on to.

Where victoria shopping centre is now, was a Railway station. The clock still stands today, next door was a large indoor market.

My mum says when she got her house in 1963 next to morley school, it cost 11 shillings a week rent, about 60p now! She went to work for Boots in their offices and she earned £5-50p per week.

Where "The chase" shops are now, large houses lined each side, where rich people lived or retired, Doctors and Lawyers and most of them had servants. About half way along St Anns Well Road was St Ann's Infant School, it was a very old building, my sister who is 30 now, went there.

Even up to 1982 when we left our old house, my mum still had an outdoor loo, a very tiny old kitchen with no units and a coal fire. She says she would love a coal fire today!

The End.

Claire's family tree. Asterisks show family members who live in St Anns. Margaret Bradbury is the Nan interviewed

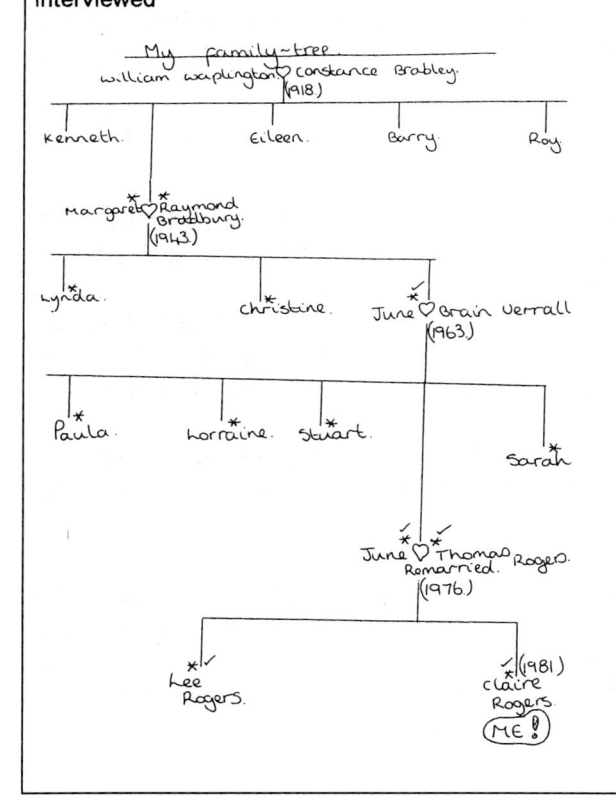

Victoria washhouse (1973) mentioned by Claire's Nan
Nottingham Corporation Baths Department
Local Studies Library, Angel Row

ANTI-BULLYING PEER COUNSELLING SCHEME.

The following information [November 1997] was on the Scheme's Internet website WWW.ndirect.co.uk/-northolmer/.

ABC was inspired by the TV documentary featuring Acland Burghly School in Camden, London. Robin Tinker and Derek Wilson, from Elliott Durham, visited that school to learn more. As a result, ABC was established in Elliott Durham in Autumn 1995, with the first counsellors trained by February 1996. Since then, Elliott Durham has been active in helping the Scheme to develop countywide.

The website message from Head Teacher, Kathy Yates, states: "We take in children with a wide range of ability from those with learning and behavioural difficulties to those who are educationally very able, and who will go on to College and University.

"We have children here from a number of ethnic groups, the largest being white British, African Caribbean and Pakistani-Muslim. Our multicultural/anti-racist policy is a powerful working document and we are proud of our community links and the friendship between students of different socio-economic and racial groups.

"However, even though our school is a very happy one, any Head Teacher who denies the existence of bullying has got a real problem! Every school contains students who are unkind to others and the skill is detecting bullying and having a number of strategies, understood by the school and the wider community, to support both the victims and the bullies.

"Here at Elliott Durham we use a number of strategies including ABC, which is a system using trained student counsellors for victims of bullying who prefer to speak to one of their peers about the problem, rather than to a member of staff. Our ABC initiative has received enormous publicity and acclaim throughout Nottinghamshire and training sessions have been run by our student counsellors for other schools."

****

The service offered is confidential and counsellors are responsible for all aspects of the service including publicity in and outside school, organisaing interviews with clients, having a key to the ABC room and unlimited access to the school on ABC business. They are supported by staff at a weekly supervision meeting. Counsellors support each other and give up considerable amounts of time to make ABC work. They have spoken to school assemblies, tutor groups, met prospective parents and pupils from local feeder schools.

In July 1997, three ABC counsellors led a County in-service training event called Peer Counselling as an Anti-bullying Strategy. For more details contact Robin Tinker or Terry Whysall.

In a Press interview [Nottingham Evening Post 22.2.97] the County's educational psychologist, Derek Wilson, said: "We have a credible group of kids we know won't let us down and now have the confidence to take it [ABC] to other schools. "It affects the whole culture of a school by giving the message that people care. Young people are under used in schools because of anxiety about sharing power with them."

Adult counsellor and Elliott Durham teacher, Robin Tinker, stated: "At first it was perceived as risky giving youngsters the power and responsibility. But they have done well. One of the top rules is confidentiality. No names are ever given at our meetings."

Student peer counsellors at November 1997. Back row (l to r) Michael Blackham (year 11), Imran Dar (year 11), Aron Birchall (year 9). Front row (l to r) Louise Brown (year 9) and Natasha Mighten (year 10)

Here are the statements they made for their ABC Internet website.

Michael Blackham : "I wanted to become a counsellor because I thought that if I could help my friends with bullying problems, maybe I could help others. I helped to lead a course called Peer Counselling as an Anti-bullying Strategy in July 1997. I spoke to teachers about ABC and what happens in our school."

Imran Dar (16): "Not only does ABC help the victims of bullying, but sometimes we help the bullies as well. I wanted to become an ABC counsellor because I was a victim of bullying and was even a bully myself. So using my experience of both situations, I thought I could help people who found themselves in either situation. ABC has improved my relationships with staff and pupils and has helped me to become a better person."

Aron Birchall (13): "My hobbies are football, cricket and swimming. I also like writing. I have four brothers called Ashley, Alex, Adam and Andrew who was one of the first ABC counsellors at Elliott Durham. I became a counsellor because my friend was being bullied and I wanted to help him. I like helping my friends."

Louise Brown (13): "I have been doing this job for almost a year. I wanted to be a counsellor because I wanted to help people, both the victims and the bullies. In July this year, I helped to lead a course for other teachers in Nottinghamshire. I really enjoyed it."

Natasha Mighten (14): "I am a very understanding person and I take time to listen to people who are bullies or who are being bullied. I know how they feel from my own experience because I have been bullied and have been a bully. I enjoy being an ABC counsellor."

GREATER NOTTINGHAM Compact

AND ELLIOTT DURHAM SCHOOL

THE FOLLOWING STUDENTS HAVE BEEN AWARDED THE COMPACT

CERTIFICATE OF DISTINCTION

LUCY ALLFREE	SHAKEEL RASUL
MARK BOND	KERRY RILEY
MICHELLE BRODRICK	SAQAB SALIM
NICOLA BROWN	LUKE THACKRAY
CALLECIA BROWN	KAREN THOMPSON
STEVEN BROWN	DAVID WALL
MARGHERITA BUBBICO	AFUA BOAFA
DANIEL ELFORD	LYNDSAY BOOTH
KELLY ELFORD	STEVEN COTTERILL
BEN GARNER	JERMAINE DUFFUS
MARK GRAHAM	BERNADETTE EARLEY
MARIE GRECO	MICHAEL HART
COLIN GREENSMITH	RYAN HARVEY
MAGSOOD HUSSAIN	LOUISE JARRETT
KELLY MORRELL	GLENN LINTON
CARRIE NEEDHAM	SHEETAL PALA
PHUOC-THI-NGUYEN	ROBERT ROSE
CLAIRE PATALA	NISBAT SALID
NATALIE PHIPPS	CLAIRE THOMPSON
EMMA PICKER	JASON WEST
SHAUN PRITCHARD	KERRY WHITCHURCH

To receive this certificate students successfully met Compact targets in:

✓ *Attendance and punctuality*

✓ *Coursework completion*

✓ *Completion of a work experience placement*

✓ *Individual goals*

and are now eligible to take advantage of Compact opportunities

SUPPORTED BY:

GREATER NOTTINGHAM TEC

Greater Nottingham Education Business Partnership

GREATER NOTTINGHAM TRAINING & ENTERPRISE COUNCIL

Date? Early 1990's?

SCHOOL UNIFORM

This has remained constant over the years, though obviously styles have changed and there have been adaptations: for example, including trousers for girls as an option.

The school stipulates that girls wear a blue or white blouse with collar; school tie (optional); plain navy V neck jumper; sweatshirt or cardigan; navy, grey or black skirt or trousers; flat black shoes.

Cultural and religious beliefs of parents and students as regards dress are respected e.g. navy blue Shalwar chemiz when appropriate.

Boys wear a blue or white shirt with collar; school tie (optional); plain navy V neck jumper or sweatshirt; grey, black or navy trousers; flat black shoes.

Raincoats, anoraks, overcoats etc: navy or black or other plain dark colours.

Sports details (opposite) and school curriculum details (right) from school information (1997)

ELLIOTT DURHAM SCHOOL

SCHOOL CURRICULUM

All pupils take English, Mathematics, Design Technology, a Modern Foreign Language, Information Technology, Balanced Science (Modular) which covers Physics, Chemistry and Biology, Personal and Social Education, Physical Education, Religious Education and a Humanities subject.

Most subjects are taken to GCSE level.

GCSE is provided through the Midland Examining Group, the Northern Examining Association and the Southern Examining Group.

Year 10 pupils in September 1997 were able to choose from the following subjects:

Art and Design	History
Design & Technology: Resistant Materials	Humanities
Technology: Systems Control	French
Design Technology: Graphic Products	Urdu
English Literature	Drama
Geography	Sports Studies
German	Media Studies
Home Economics: Child Development	

CAREERS EDUCATION AND GUIDANCE

Careers Education and Guidance is all about helping young people to make informed choices about their life when they leave school at sixteen.

The school has a Careers Education Policy which is available on request.

We work very closely with Guideline Career Services to ensure all pupils in their last year have an impartial guidance interview.

Most pupils who leave Elliott Durham carry on with their education at one of the local colleges. We have very close links with the colleges and all young people in the school have an opportunity to visit a college.

At the end of year 10 and again at the beginning of year 11 all pupils are offered a work experience placement. This placement gives the pupils a chance to understand what happens at work.

Contact.

ELLIOTT DURHAM SCHOOL COMMUNITY NEWSLETTER
Serving the St Anns and Mapperley Areas

The Big Bash!

On 29th November 48 year 8 students had a thoroughly enjoyable time at The BBC Big Bash at the NEC Birmingham. Those who were feeling energetic played basketball, hockey, rugby and football with some of England's top sporting stars. Others gazed adoringly at the new up and coming talent in the British pop world. There were lots of opportunities for hands-on and technological activities with the Blue Peter and Smart team, amongst others. After an exhausting day, staff were thanked by all the students who only had one complaint,

"Do we have to go home now? - Let's stay 'till tomorrow."

Three items from CONTACT, the newsy A5 newsletter which started Summer 1996 (alas issues not yet dated!)

Girls Football

Girls are proving that football is as much a game for them as it is for boys, with successes coming in both city and county competitions. The under 12 squad were recent finalists in the Nottingham Schools' 5 a side final. The under 13 age group has recently qualified for the quarter finals of the County Cup by beating Dayncourt School by 4 goals to 2, with a hat trick being scored by Charlene Simmons. The team meet Haywood School in the next round. The under 14 squad, not wanting to be left out, reached the finals of the City Cup. They did this by going through the north of the city qualifying rounds undefeated.

Elliott Durham Christmas Road Show.

Fourteen year 8 students and their English teachers entertained students at Walter Halls, Blue Bell Hill, Sycamore, Elms, Huntingdon and Morley Primary Schools. The six shows included a specially adapted version of William Shakespeare's "Romeo and Juliet" mind-reading, jokes, songs, the ever popular 'lose your onion' quiz, and a well choreographed pop mime of The Spice Girls. There was something for everybody, popular and classical; a variety performance which displayed the marvellous talents of Elliott Durham students and their teachers and brought hours of entertainment to each of the family feeder schools.

ELLIOTT DURHAM SCHOOL
TEACHING STAFF LIST (September 1997)

Andrews, Dave	Head of House/Drama/English	DA
Blackmore, Peter	Head of Learning Support	PB
Boothroyd, Rob	Deputy Head Teacher/Humanities	RB
Bowden, Dennis	Maths	DB
Bromley, Sandra	Assistant Head of House/PE	SB
Crouch, Dave	Acting Head of English	DC
Duflot, Annette	Assistant Head of House/Modern Languages	AD
Daffé, Jane	Section XI - Language Support	JD
Finn, Annie	Creative Studies	AF
Fowler, Joy	Head of House/Food Technology	JF
Harris, Gary	Humanities	GH
Hendry, Ron	Head of PE	RH
Johnson, Ian	Head of Humanities	IJ
Jones, Sue	English	SJ
Knock, Dave	Head of Mathematics	DK
Legg, Colin	Science	CL
Lilley, Antoinette	Section XI/Achievement Project	AL
Major, Gerald	Assistant Head of House/Second in Mathematics	GM
McIntyre, Jo	Acting Second in English/Media Studies	JM
Murphy, Linda	Head of Modern Languages	LM
Nelson, Annette	Section XI Consultant/Home School Links	AN
Pidgeon, Fred	Technical Graphics/Technology	FP
Posner, Naomi	Modern Languages	NP
Raoof, Gazala	Urdu	GR
Rutherford, Rose	Art	RR
Simmons, Tony	Maths	TS
Stimson, Chris	Head of House/Science	CS
Stimson, Rick	Head of Science	RS
Tinker, Robin	Head of PSE/Integrated Humanities	RT
Whitby, Pat	Co-ordinator of Industry Links/Careers/Food Tech	PW
White, Moira	Second in Science	MW
Whysall, Terry	Deputy Head Teacher/English	TW
Wood, Claire	Maths	CW
Wright, Stuart	Head of IT/Exam Co-ordinator	SW
Yates, Kathy	Head Teacher/Humanities	KY

Elliott Durham has a caring and hard working staff who are committed to motivate pupils and to encourage their success and development. The school ethos is characterised by concern and respect for others. Pupils display loyalty to the school and positive attitudes to its community and environment.

School Inspector's Report 1994.

MEMBERS OF THE GOVERNING BODY - 1997/98

NAME	APPOINTING BODY
Mr A Shepherd	LEA
County Councillor Burgess	LEA
Councillor Mrs B Higgins	LEA
Mrs M Snowden	LEA
Vacancy	Co-option
Mr K S Ubhi	Co-option
Mrs L Miller	Co-option
County Councillor M Edwards	Co-option
Mr D Blain	Co-option
Mrs R Taylor	Parent
Mr Wheatcroft	Parent
Mrs J Todd	Parent
Mrs C Brown	Parent
Mrs C Stimson	Teaching
Mr S Wright	Teaching
Mrs K J Yates	Head Teacher

ANCILLIARY STAFF

LIBRARIAN	Lynne Fielding
SCHOOL OFFICE	Linda Miller
	Gail Palethorpe
SCHOOL OFFICE/RESOURCES	Glynis Scorer
SNSA	Adrian Dyer
EWO	Janet Wardle
TECHNICIANS	Bina Holmes
	Jill Gross
SCHOOL NURSE	Margaret Hopkins
CARETAKING STAFF	Site Manager: Patrick Belshaw
	Kevin Young

ELLIOTT DURHAM SCHOOL

SPORT

The school sports department aims to provide a wide range of enjoyable sporting opportunities for ALL students. Competitive activities in both team and individual sports are encouraged and offered to students together with opportunities for recreational activities.

Examination courses in GCSE PE are also offered by graduate Physical Education Specialists. National Coaching Qualifications in the following areas are held by staff:

- Basketball
- Badminton
- Swimming
- Trampolining
- Athletics
- Football
- Hockey
- Canoeing
- Hill Walking

The team sports of Football, Cricket, Hockey and Basketball are played on a regular inter-school basis by both boys and girls. The school enjoys regular success in the City Leagues whilst also participating in County competitions. The school is also represented in the City Cross Country and Athletics meetings. Inter-house sport is a feature of the sporting ethos of the school, together with the traditional Schools Sports Day and Swimming Gala.

At both Key Stage 3 and Key Stage 4 the curriculum covers the activity areas of games, athletics, gym, swimming and dance. At Key Stage 4 the students also have the opportunity to use off site facilities.

The students enjoy a wide range of sports clubs that are available both during dinner times and after school. These include: Football, Basketball, Badminton, Hockey, Tennis, Trampolining, Cricket, Canoeing, Cross-Country, Athletics and Aerobics. These clubs are provided by staff within the school and by fully qualified staff from the City Challenge Team, with whom we have an excellent liaison programme. The school is also a site for the No Limits programme providing activities for the community and is a satellite club for Magdala Tennis Club.

The school has excellent sports facilities. Inside there is a Sports Hall with a full size basketball court, 4 badminton courts and areas for gymnastics, indoor football, netball and hockey. There is also a small carpeted hall for dance and aerobics. Outside there are 4 tennis courts, 2 floodlit astro-turf areas and extensive playing fields. There is also a swimming pool on the school campus, used by the school and the community.

Above: students visit the Nottingham Evening Post to watch the special Elliott Durham supplement being prepared (see also pages 6 & 56). Nottingham Evening Post photo archive. July 1984

Nottinghamshire County Council Education
Nottinghamshire Education Committee
School Holidays 1998/99
(1st September 1998 - 31st August 1999 inclusive)

■ School Holiday ▨ Administration Day (staff only) ▧ Bank Holiday

This pattern gives 195 working days for staff including the administration day, Monday 7th September 1998. A total of 4 in-service training days for staff will be taken by each school from the 194 term days given above, leaving 190 term days for pupils.

ELLIOTT DURHAM SCHOOL

SCHOOL DAY BEGINS	8.55 AM
MORNING BREAK	11.15 AM - 11.30 AM
LUNCH	12.25 PM - 1.25 PM
CHANGE OVER BELL	2.25 PM - 2.30 PM
SCHOOL DAY ENDS	3.25 PM

TIMES OF LESSONS

PERIOD	
1	9.25 AM - 10.20 AM
2	10.20 AM - 11.15 AM
3	11.30 AM - 12.25 PM
4	1.30 PM - 2.25 PM
5	2.30 PM - 3.25 PM

On entry to Elliott Durham, students [1997] are allocated to one of three Houses, Edmonton, Lawrence and Vancouver. As the school became smaller Hudson, Ottawa and Toronto Houses were put 'on hold.' Each House consists of 'vertical' tutor sets which includes a mix of students from each of the five year groups.

Some more details of Elliott Durham' life now (which may look quite different 10-20 years on?)

REFLECTIONS OF THE CURRENT HEAD TEACHER.

Sometimes it feels as if I have been at Elliott Durham for ever, at others it seems like yesterday. I had to look up the date when I first arrived, says Kathy Yates.

I joined the School in September 1985 as a Deputy Head. At that time, there were over 800 children in the school and it always seemed very crowded and noisy. Now, with only 450 children on roll we have a lot more space to move around in. I prefer running a small school. You get to know all the children personally.

I remember my first day very clearly. In my previous school I had taught 20 lessons out of 25. As a Deputy I had only a teaching timetable of 12 lessons a week. So, after the staff briefing on the first morning, I left the staffroom thinking: "I wonder what I do now?" because I wasn't teaching for the rest of the day. I needn't have worried, because when I got to my room there was a queue of parents with their children waiting to be admitted to the school. By the time I had finished with them and the associated paperwork, the day was over.

Since that time, I can honestly say there has never been a moment when I have felt bored or had nothing to do. Elliott Durham will always be a friendly, busy school with a lot going on.

In September 1990, I became Acting Head Teacher when Mr Bailey was seconded to County Hall to work on financial management. This was only meant to be for a year but he then applied for a Headship at Harry Carlton School, got the job and never came back!

I was interviewed for the permanent post in 1991 and although I had never planned or wanted to 'get to the top,' found myself in that position. During these five years of Headship the changes to the education system have been enormous. They have been so extensive and turbulent that I am sure the job of Head Teacher would be unrecognisable to former heads like Mr Davies.

Local Management of schools, the National Curriculum, SATS, Vocational Qualifications, Records of Achievement and Appraisal are only some of the initiatives which schools have had to cope with. Parental choice and the power of Governors has led to schools becoming increasingly accountable for such things as exam results, truancy statistics and exclusion figures. We now need written policies for just about everything. And who had heard of an OFSTED inspection five years ago?

Since the age of 21, when I first started teaching, I have always worked in inner-city schools: it was where I wanted to be. Some parents have asked me if I will ever move to another school (I hope this is because they want me to stay!) but I would like to end where I started.

Elliott Durham's Danny Frings, one of five Nottingham students, selected through an International Youth Education Project run by Worldrite, to travel to Ghana in Summer 1997. Danny, who has now left school, has shared his experiences of Africa since his return through talks and slide shows

Nottingham Evening Post

LOCAL HISTORY PROJECT (continued from pages 57-62). Twenty three students 'brainstormed' the things they like and dislike about St Anns. Then these likes and dislikes were discussed and positive suggestions made. Here is a synopsis.

LIKE ST ANNS BECAUSE:-

* There are lots of shops, and shops nearby. [This view is interesting because older people like those, for example, attending the annual Reminiscence Days in St Anns Library look back with longing to the many and varied shops which were lost when the old St Anns was pulled down. Ed] Year 9 students felt St Anns is much better off for local shops than many areas.
* St Anns is near the City Centre. They like the freedom of being able to walk to the Centre.
* Sycamore Sports Centre. Good facilities but many in the class feel it is too far from where they live in St Anns.
* Schools. General satisfaction with their experience of Primary Schools and of Elliott Durham.

DISLIKE ST ANNS BECAUSE:-

* It has a bad reputation. This grievance cropped up time and again throughout the local history sessions. It is felt not to be fair.
* Pollution, graffiti, scruffiness. Agreed that pollution isn't limited to St Anns. More people could take pride in keeping the estate shipshape. But that went for many areas.
* Too many hills and the speed ramps on the Wells Road. Well, that's the way it is!
* Overcrowded. Obviously when compared to the old St Anns, there are fewer people. Yet it seems crowded, but no idea why this should be except a clear feeling that there is a lot of 'useless' space around. This was space which was just 'there.' It couldn't be used for anything. For example: "No ball games allowed." This sort of space coupled with the very symmetrical layout of the estate made it seem crowded and impersonal.
* Not enough places to go. For example, not enough tennis courts, and the football field is hogged by gangs or by elderly people. A general feeling of frustration. Several students go to amenities (e.g. sports centres) outside the area.
* Things cost too much. Agreed, this is not specific to St Anns.
* Not enough jobs. A feeling fed by experience of others, often family members, that having a St Anns address creates more problems in finding work than is fair.

POSITIVE SUGGESTIONS:-

* Lots of people should write to the Council about their ideas for improving things.
* Need to change the bad reputation and image of St Anns.
* Need public transport serving the estate in addition to the main routes through it.
* Need a good park which could always be used.
* Need more Police and Neighbourhood Watch Schemes.
* Need somewhere, with competent adult help, to do handicrafts, sports etc. Want to learn things, not just to be 'contained.'

Some of these ideas were looked at in more detail, together with details Ruth introduced about the history of St Anns, including co-operative ventures. For example, a Street Warden Scheme experiment, the Fair Heating Campaign had a positive outcome, local people succeeded in getting the Caunton Avenue flats demolished. Local co-operation had prevented an Inner Ring Road cutting through the 'new' St Anns, particular religious and community organisations ran activities which met the needs of various groups, St Anns was proud of its Library at the bottom of Robin Hood Chase...

St Anns Local Plan Review, Nottingham Corporation, January 1986, stated: "St Anns contains a wide variety of community facilities..." These were listed in an Appendix. The students said the list looked impressive to outsiders but did not really offer so much. One student said with some passion that until she was six she went to a youth group on the list. "We said prayers, played games, stitched: always just the same. We didn't learn anything." As a change, she once went to ballet classes at Blue Bell Hill Community Centre. "I looked ridiculous [because she grew early] and felt ridiculous. Some would like these things, but we can't all fit in but we do have ideas," she said.

These young people would welcome more adults who could share interesting skills. For example, in a Bicycle Club, rock climbing, abseiling, roller skating, and craft skills, learning 'real' skills, not simply being kept 'occupied.'

They suggested that it should be possible to use the School's premises and playing fields more often out of school hours for regular activities with experienced adults to run them. They didn't expect teachers to do this after their day's work. They realised funds would be needed but it was stupid that the school's well-equipped premises and sports fields should be so little used out of school hours.

Because the School was on top of the hill, some transport would be needed to get home after dark. It wasn't their fault the School wasn't in the middle of St Anns. Some of the group gave a lot of detailed thought about how activities could be run [which, of course, they are in some Comprehensive Schools which have been built integrally with Leisure and Community Centres].

One student wanted an opportunity (perhaps via a Questionnaire) to ask the Boots plc staff at its Headquarters in Nottingham what they thought of St Anns. There was insufficient time to take this idea further. It was a positive idea toward encouraging a group of employed people to put forward their ideas about St Anns and for the young people of St Anns to be able to meet some of them to discuss these ideas.

WHOSE HISTORY IS CORRECT?

Students considered the need not to believe statements without carefully examining them. Differing accounts of local situations were considered. For example, the Community Craft Centre experiment in Blue Bell Hill, St Anns, which ran for several years just prior to demolition.

A group of young people lived in a commune and worked without pay or State benefit payments. Local shopkeepers provided their food and they paid a peppercorn rent. They ran a lunch club with a free meal for elders, helped in the playground, cleaned chimneys, mended doors, ran a craft centre, had a clothes exchange shop. In short they offered a practical experiment of how community self-help, exchange of skills, and barter can work in the modern world.

Ray Gosling, co-founder and Chairman of the St Anns Tenants' and Residents' Association at the time of the 'old' St Anns demise, was one of the people who held these hard working young people in high esteem. Some others strongly criticised them publicy. 'For' and 'against' accounts were studied. The Elliott Durham students concluded that those who spoke against the experiment "were jealous."

[Elliott Durham pupils had helped with the making of a film about the Community Craft Centre, see Page 16. Accounts of the Centre can be found in old Chase Chats and in St Anns News which preceded Chase Chat. Also in Ray Gosling's <u>Personal Copy: A Memoir of the Sixties,</u> Faber & Faber, 1980]

Another case study of **whose history is correct** were two stories about St Anns told by people Ruth interviewed the previous week. They both live in the same part of St Anns. The first was trying to leave St Anns. Young lads were breaking in at all hours. Nobody was willing to take responsibility in the neighbourhood in case of reprisals. The shed went and: "Nobody saw it. Unless people work together, it will get worse and worse," she said.

The second said she had, at last, managed to come back to St Anns. She did this because St Anns was so friendly. "You live alone but do not feel lonely. You can walk where you need to go."

The group felt that people would want to believe the first account. Yes, such things happened but not nearly as often as people made out and they were often talked up. And, when they did happen, there *were* things which could be done to improve matters. What? Better lighting; cutting off 'useless run through' routes; being taken more seriously when things were reported. If there were more things 'to go to,' there would be more people out and about which would make people feel safer. And lads breaking in was <u>not</u> only happening in St Anns.

****

YOU DESERVE TO BE REMEMBERED

Write your own life story - send for your own copy of RUTH'S ARCHIVE special fill-in book* on archive quality paper.

The fill-in book helps you to write about the many happenings which 'ordinary' people experience and/or undertake and which too often get totally taken for granted. We call these things community activity because they are the building blocks of everyday life in local communities (even though people often do not think of them as 'activities').

The fill-in book provides an explanatory structure but allows you to write in any way you like. There is no 'correct' way. Many older people have found writing 'their' book to be a real pleasure and life affirming.

RUTH'S ARCHIVE fill-in books, when completed, are returned to become part of a permanent ARCHIVE which will help future generations understand our times. You can add your life story to this ARCHIVE if you live anywhere in the UK, or if you have lived in the UK at any time of your life.

UK £6.00 (post free) from

RUTH'S ARCHIVE P O BOX 66 WARWICK CV34 4XE